Doubt To Certainty

Also By M. E. Wasfi

The Human Malfunction

The Laws of the Time

Beyond Performance Metrics

Doubt To Certainty

*A Practical Guide To Finding Confidence
and Clarity In Making Complex Decisions*

M. E. Wasfi

Doubt To Certainty: A Practical Guide To Finding Confidence and Clarity In Making Complex Decisions

Copyright © 2025 M.E. Wasfi

For permissions, licensing inquiries, or bulk orders, contact:
IVIC Decisions FZCO
Email: info@ivicdecisions.com
Website: https://ivicdecisions.com

ISBN (Paperback): 979-8864139240

Amazon Kindle Direct Publishing (KDP) Edition

Published & distributed worldwide through Amazon Kindle Direct Publishing

Printed in the United States of America and other countries by Amazon KDP's global print network

Dedication

I dedicate this book to you.

Segment Directory

Doubt To Certainty

Acknowledgment

The journey to creating this book has been one that is both deeply personal and profoundly shaped by the influences of a few pivotal entities and individuals. Writing this acknowledgment is a heartfelt tribute to those who have made a significant impact on this work. Their contributions have been invaluable in transforming a dream into the pages you hold today.

First and foremost, the People Dynamics Learning Group deserves a special mention. Based in Canada, this organization has played an instrumental role in molding the perspectives that shape much of my mindset as a person and a coach, and thus this book's content. The commitment of this institution to fostering continuous learning is something I am forever grateful for. Beyond their foundational influence on me as a learner, the leadership team at People Dynamics Learning Group generously devoted their time to review this manuscript and provide insights. To them, I owe a deep sense of gratitude for being a beacon of knowledge and enlightenment.

Now, speaking of influences that may seem fleeting but are lasting in their impact, I recall the brief yet monumental interaction I had with Ashraf Helal, the Founder of Helal CMC in Egypt. Ashraf and I crossed paths during a leadership development program. We met just once, virtually, but the spark of that singular meeting ignited a series of discussions and collaborations that played a crucial role in this book's evolution. Ashraf's openness to dialogue and his generosity in sharing insights stand out vividly in my memory. His feedback was strategic and technical, all focused on refining perspectives and coaching approaches. Every thinker dreams of meeting someone who pushes them to look deeper, and with Ashraf, I found just that guiding force. For his generous contribution of time, expertise, and relentless encouragement, I offer my heartfelt thanks.

Jos Burton's name was one I stumbled upon serendipitously. An esteemed coach, lecturer, and author himself, Jos had no prior connection to me. On a whim, I reached out to him on LinkedIn, presenting my first draft and seeking his unbiased first impression. In a world where time is premium and expertise even more so, Jos' willingness to dive into my work with such meticulous attention left me both humbled and immensely grateful. His feedback was akin to shining a light in dark corners, making me see the nuances I had missed, and grounding me in objectivity and positivity. With his insights, I was better equipped to tackle the core challenges and craft coherent solutions, and his feedback taught me to think more inclusively and objectively. His actions reminded me of the power of genuine collaboration even when it springs from the most unexpected sources. To Jos, I owe a renewed sense of purpose as an author and a reminder of the inherent generosity that exists within the writing community. Looking forward to meeting you in UK, Jos!

As I ventured deeper into the writing process and approached the last steps of editing the book, I realized that crafting a compelling narrative was only one facet of creating a book. Turning those narratives into a product that resonates with readers required a different kind of guidance. Enter Habib Chammas. Habib, the three-time bestselling author, was the lighthouse I did not know I needed. Habib is based in Dubai, and was in Lebanon when I first reached out to him. With the same generosity with which he pens his books, he shared his vast knowledge and experiences with me. He was not just guiding me on the technicalities of book creation, but went beyond to ensure that the end product is both relevant and impactful. It is rare to find someone who willingly parts with their hard-earned wisdom to uplift another, and in Habib, I found that rare gem. To him, I owe more than just thanks - I owe the clarity and precision this book has been able to achieve.

Back to Canada, special thanks to my dear colleague and friend, Margaret Gustavel. Marg, with her laser-focused insights and generous allocation of time, has been an invaluable compass in navigating the creation of this book. It's one thing to have a sea of ideas, and entirely another to organize them into a coherent, engaging structure. That's precisely what Marg's advice empowered me to do. She provided the clarity needed to finalize the book's outline and bring forth its substance in the most impactful way. With every discussion, Marg sifted through layers of thought and intricacy and made sure the core essence of this book shone through clearly. So here is to Marg, whose keen eye and sage advice have immeasurably shaped this book's direction. Her contributions will forever resonate in the pages of this book, and -by extension- in the lives that this book touches.

Lastly, sincere gratitude to my coaching clients, for they have been the real heroes in this journey. My clients are based in, and come from, all 7 inhabited continents, and they are the beating heart of the narrative and methodologies introduced in this book. Entrusting me with piloting the IVIC Decision-Making Framework© and the Authenticity Pyramid©, they were the brave souls who stepped into uncharted waters, allowing themselves to be guided by coaching processes still in their nascent stages of development. Their feedback, experiences, and transformative journeys stand as living testimonials to these models' effectiveness. The fact that you, the reader, can now benefit from a validated coaching methodology is a testament to their faith, resilience, and openness to change. They enriched it with their inputs and validated its power. Their trust - in both the coaching process and in me - bestowed me with the confidence to consolidate these thoughts and present them to the world in the form of this book. Their journeys, filled with discoveries and transformations, are the best endorsements of the ideas contained within these pages. Their belief transformed nascent ideas into powerful methodologies, and for that, they have my endless appreciation. I will refrain from mentioning specific names to honor the confidentiality agreements I have with them. To each one of them, I owe a debt of gratitude that words can barely encapsulate.

While this book carries my name on its spine, the influences, support, and guidance of these partners have been fundamental to its creation. To the People Dynamics Learning Group, Ashraf Helal, Jos Burton, Habib Chammas, Margaret Gustavel, and all my coaching clients – my heartfelt gratitude for being the wind beneath this book's wings. Your belief, feedback, and generosity have truly made this journey memorable, and this product meaningful. Here is to every discussion, critique, and shared insight – they have, in no small measure, made this book what it is.

Declaration

Some of the characters, organizations, locations, and other identities mentioned as case studies have been changed to avoid legal conflicts. These modifications will have no impact on the argument. All clients' case studies shared in this book are real

and authentic professional experiences.

Introduction

Life is three days: a day you cannot bring back, a day you are not aware of, and a day that you know nothing about.

I. Decisions, what are they?

What do you mean by your life when you allude to it this way? I often wonder when I hear someone say, "I want my life to be like this or that," or "I want this person in my life," or even more generally, "Why is life so hard?" or "life is beautiful!". What do you mean by the word life? One argument is that life's definition is the existence on planet Earth. But then, how about different worldviews that entail the belief in an afterlife? An afterlife is still life, isn't it? Some talk about life as a voyage filled with memorable experiences, relationships, and personal growth. Others view it through a spiritual lens, where concepts like the afterlife give life a deeper, more eternal meaning. Life, you see, is more than a biological phenomenon. Sure, it is about existing on planet Earth, breathing, eating, and doing all those things that living beings do. But does not it seem like there is something more to it?

The literal meaning of life can be as diverse as the people pondering it. Whether it is the scientific terminology of existence, the philosophical pursuit of purpose, or the spiritual connection to something greater, life's meaning can be multifaceted and profoundly personal. What is the hidden beauty of it? You get to decide

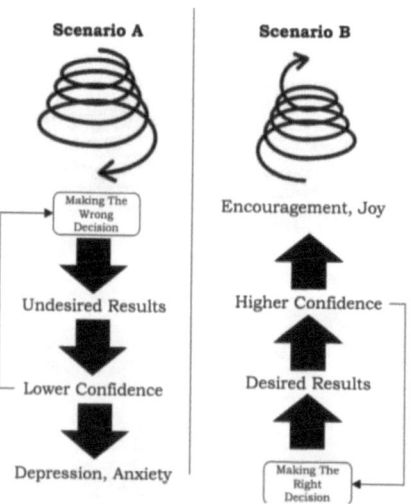

Scenario A

Making The Wrong Decision

Undesired Results

Lower Confidence

Depression, Anxiety

Scenario B

Encouragement, Joy

Higher Confidence

Desired Results

Making The Right Decision

what life means to you, and that is a decision as empowering and unique as you are. And this is my own definition of life: Decisions. To me, life = Decisions. Let me explain.

When I think about the world and observe how it moves and changes, I see two things driving it all – human decisions, and nature's decisions. One person's decision is essentially the input for you to make a decision of your own, and a nature's decision would have the same impact on you. This idea, The Butterfly Effect, is what Edward Lorenz articulated in 1972. Lorenz is a mathematician and a meteorologist who brought this concept to life, showing us how something as small as the flap of a butterfly's wings could lead to something as significant as a tornado on the other side of the world.

In its essence, The Butterfly Effect is a chaos theory explaining how those small changes in a system can lead to huge differences in their outcome. Let us take a human decision, such as planting a tree in your backyard. This simple gesture does more than beautify your surroundings; it actually contributes to cleaner air. According to NASA, one tree can absorb up to 48 pounds of carbon dioxide annually.

Now, imagine your community of people making a collective decision, where everyone in your town plants a tree. That would be a global contribution to a healthier environment. For a change in context, consider a business decision to reduce plastic usage in a small café in Japan. This decision might inspire and push other local businesses and lead to a significant reduction in single-use plastics. That traffic light you sit at itself is a result of a decision - a city planner's choice, made years ago, to manage traffic flow. And here you are, responding to it by stopping or moving. The meal you had for breakfast is a combination of a farmer's decision to grow a specific crop, a chef's decision to create a recipe, and even the weather's "decision" to provide the proper growing conditions. Every bite you took was a culmination of numerous decisions, many beyond your control, shaping your experience. Every choice you make, or think you are making, is determined by countless variables.

See? People make simple decisions, and these decisions reach you to consequently make decisions of your own. You, in turn, make a simple decision, and you end up impacting yourself, others, and nature. You may find it fascinating how decisions, both by humans and nature, can create ripples that affect everything around them.

Speaking of nature, a volcanic eruption in Iceland, like the one in Eyjafjallajökull in 2010, led to a cloud of ash that affected air travel across Europe. According to the International Air Transport Association, this natural event disrupted 90,000 flights and affected millions of passengers. Nature's decision to erupt a volcano impacted human decisions across an entire continent. In another continent, a natural occurrence of a prolonged drought in Sub-Saharan Africa might lead to food and water scarcity, affecting millions of people's livelihoods. The World Food Programme stated that in 2019, more than 45 million people in the region were facing severe food shortages due to drought. In your own world, if it rains while you have planned to go jogging, you will have a decision to make: whether you still want to stick to your plan, adjust it, or cancel it.

The world you inhabit and the life you lead are a continuous dance of decisions and reactions, a blend of human choice and nature's way, all interwoven in the most complex and fascinating way. This is the world you reside in, with its dynamics and forces at play. Your decisions, and nature's, all weave into this intricate tapestry of existence. You are at the end of other people's, and nature's, decisions, and your decisions are merely responses to the repercussions of those two facts. Even if you believe you are making a decision based on an idea you got, generated from an intrinsic motive to do something, this stream of consciousness has probably been inspired by an external factor as well. You have probably heard or seen something, and this information is processed in your brain until it generates an idea. And therefore, what stimulates you to make a decision is essentially an external factor.

And so, how can we define and interpret the decisions you make? Simply put, these are your responses to the stimuli we have discussed. Suppose we define the repercussions and results of people's and nature's decisions as information. In that case, your decisions become a product of how you perceive the information, feel about them, and choose to respond to them. Consequently, your response becomes someone else's information; now, the ball is in their court to make a decision, and so on. This is how I see my life, and I encourage you to see yours as a product of your responses to these stimuli. Now you understand how the quality of your decisions shapes the quality of your life. Every choice you make is a paint brush stroke, creating a visual representation and a unique portrait of your existence. When you tap into your values, goals, and information, you consciously control how the image looks, and it becomes vibrant, vivid, and alive. On the other hand, making choices hastily, impulsively, or in a state of stress, shakes your hand and the colors blur, creating a mess.

Decisions are a fascinating combo of conscious reasoning and unconscious instincts, varying in complexity, intricacy, and nature. They can be diversified into different categories, each with its own distinctive attributes and methodologies. In some situations, decisions are like day-to-day routines, like choosing what to wear or eat. These often do not require much contemplation but are crucial to your daily functioning. On the other end of the spectrum are strategic decisions. These are big-picture choices, often requiring critical analysis and meticulous examination. They might include deciding on a career path or launching a new product line. When making these decisions, you are likely to spend adequate time gathering information, analyzing risks, and considering their long-term aftermaths. This is a widely popular and highly regarded method employed in business and personal growth planning, where substantial investments of time and resources are at stake. Between these two extremes lie tactical decisions. These are usually short-term choices that are more complex and convoluted than routine decisions but do not carry the weight of strategic decisions. As an illustration, deciding how to approach a work project or planning a family holiday falls into this category.

The way you approach making these decisions is a different story. One way of decision-making involves intuitive decisions. This is when you trust your gut feeling, past experiences, or subconscious epiphanies. You might use this when choosing a piece of art that resonates with you or even when selecting a life partner. Some other decisions require ethics to be involved, and this is when you intentionally weigh moral principles and societal norms to make the decision you find suitable. For instance, business leaders often encounter ethical dilemmas that require a careful balance between profit and principles. Another way you could be making your decisions is weighing them against your values, because they are deeply personal and you want to ensure you make a decision that aligns with your core beliefs and principles. When you decide to follow a specific lifestyle, like becoming vegetarian or committing to environmental sustainability, you are making a value-based decision.

You are at a bustling marketplace in Marrakech, trying to decide which exotic spice to buy for your next culinary adventure. That is a personal decision influenced by your taste preferences, cooking style, or even the memory of a dish you once enjoyed. These personal decisions are often guided by feelings, intuition, and past experiences.

Now, shift gears and think about your career. You are in a modern office, weighing the pros and cons of two job offers. It is no longer about taste or memory but about career growth, salary, company culture, and how that aligns with your professional goals. Being there is a professional decision driven by logic, facts, and careful evaluation of multiple components. On the other hand, imagine sitting with your partner and planning your future together. You are making a decision to move in together or choosing a school for your child. These relationship decisions involve emotions, shared goals, and the delicate balance of different individual needs and views. It is like composing a duet where two musicians need to be in harmony. Shift gears again, and picture yourself in a boardroom. You are faced with strategic business decisions, like expanding into a new market or merging with a competitor. This is like playing chess on a global scale, where every move requires calculations, risk assessment, and the analysis of potential rewards. Lastly, consider managing your finances, choosing between saving, investing, or spending. Financial decisions often feel like navigating through a big city's bustling financial district, where every alleyway represents a different investment opportunity or risk. These choices need an amalgam of financial acumen, an understanding of market trends, and awareness of your financial goals and risk tolerance.

The point I am trying to make? It is that I find the way you make decisions in these different domains overlap and intertwine, fascinating! Your personal values might shape your business ethics, and your professional experiences might influence your personal relationships. Your decisions are like threads woven into the fabric of your life, each one adding color, texture, and pattern. life does not come with a manual, and decisions do not often come with clear-cut answers. So, how does it work?

II. The Reason You Doubt

Winston Churchill, the indomitable leader who led Britain through the darkest days of World War II, faced an excruciating dilemma in 1940. The British Army was trapped at Dunkirk, and the decision he had to make was both complex and crucial. Should he negotiate peace terms with Adolf Hitler or rally the country to fight on, potentially to the last man? Churchill hesitated, his mind and heart torn between the choices. A decision like this, my friend, is a clash of values, beliefs, and the heavy weight of historical consequences. And what got me wondering is: How would such an experienced and capable leader doubt? I found the answers at the very core of human nature. We face decisions every day, from mundane to life-changing, but it is the ones we consider important that compel us to pause. The reason? We give too much attention to the outcome.

When you are deeply attached to a specific outcome, the stakes of the decision become higher, and you become more hesitant. The attachment makes the decision feel weighty and significant and amplifies the fear of making a wrong choice. This anxiety then translates into skepticism and hesitancy and further clouds your judgment. Say you are leading a critical project at work, and your career advancement is perceived to hinge on its success. Since you are so attached and deeply devoted to the positive outcome, the decisions related to the project may become fraught with anxiety and self-doubt. You may second-guess your choices, fearing that one wrong move could derail the entire endeavor. In a personal context, consider a decision about relocating to a new city for a relationship. If you are intensely attached to the relationship's success, the decision to move becomes loaded with significance. Doubts creep in as you ponder every possible scenario, and the fear of "what if it does not work out?" may paralyze your decision-making process. Attachment to a specific outcome creates a tunnel vision, where only one result is viewed as acceptable or favorable to you. This rigidity limits your ability to see alternative paths and effects, and leads to increased stress and decreased confidence in your decision-making capabilities.

If decisions are responses to external stimuli, then the picture does not contain enough information. It is like trying to navigate your way in a room with little lighting. Or, on the other hand, there is too much information, and you can feel overwhelmed by a barrage of facts, opinions, and options. It can tire you out, leaving you stuck and unable to choose. Also, the future's uncertainty does not help, does it? Your decisions are predictions, like bets on what is to come in the near future. Emotional obstacles like fear, stress, anxiety, and cognitive biases make the process seem almost dizzying. Add self-doubt and societal pressures to all of these, and you have got a recipe for indecision. With these complications, life still does not slow down for you. You face conflicting values and goals, time constraints, and uncomfortable ambiguities. Our world is complicated, and right or wrong is often blurred. This complexity, coupled with fears and uncertainties, reflects our human condition. You may feel the pull between two difficult choices, something like leaving a stable job for a new opportunity, moving to a new city for love, or a decision about hiring or firing.

Scientifically, doubt is a cognitive struggle within your brain, as per a study by the University of Rochester. When doubt creeps in, your brain often sticks with what is known and familiar. It is a survival mechanism. A 2021 survey by The Decision Lab showed that 40% of respondents had avoided significant life decisions due to fear of failure. Your upbringing, experiences, and even genetics influence your approach to complex decisions. Cognitive biases further complicate your thinking. Each choice feels like a potential path with high stakes, making your mind work overtime with the "what ifs." Your life is a collection of decisions you have made and a series of calculated steps, each leading you to where you are at the present moment. This, my friend, is the challenging yet rewarding decision-making journey, uniquely yours, filled with insights and revelations that only you can uncover.

You see, decision-making is the heartbeat of life pulsing through every facet, from the deeply personal to the wide-ranging professional. You, no matter where you are in the world or what stage of life you are in, are a complex being wired for connections and relationships. Your ability to speak your language, understand your culture, and the way your thoughts form, is shaped by those around you. you have learned to feel what others feel because you naturally connect with them on an emotional level. you have likely noticed how you perceive the emotions of others, whether laughing along with a comedy show on British TV or feeling the tension during a football match in South Africa. This might remind a sports fan in Argentina of the thrill of winning the World Cup or a comedy lover in the U.S. who loves to watch Friends. We refer to it as empathy in action, and scientific studies confirm that children (you and I at some point in our lives) develop these empathic abilities between the ages of one and three. This social nature equips you with empathy, but also makes you vulnerable to manipulation. We see a strong influence in the areas of marketing and viral trends, explaining why certain advertisements, memes, or viral videos affect you. It is quite apparent and scientific how consumers are swayed by a celebrity-endorsed product and how inspirational youth are drawn into these viral social media challenges. You resonate with the emotions and moods of others, and by doing so, it allows marketers to use this to their advantage.

I remember reading about Antarctic explorers and how isolation could lead them to lose their sense of reality. that is an extreme example, but it illustrates our need for connection. However, there is a challenging side to this connection: the pressure to conform. The need for connection can sometimes push you to conform, even when it is against your true self. A young professional might feel compelled to follow corporate norms even when they clash with his personal values. let us talk about something universal: the desire to connect with something big, something sublime. It is a human thing that transcends cultures and age groups, leading to growth like pursuing art in France or martial arts in China. An entrepreneur in Nigeria might find purpose in building a community-centered business. However, it can also lead to addiction or false excitement, especially if marketing experts or social media platforms try to manipulate you.

You see, deep inside you is your true self; with a strong will and personality to make your own choices. You believe your good lies in a path, but get hesitant when you realize this path is not everyone else's choice. This is when you start thinking, "Well, maybe they are right?". You doubt because you are attached to the outcome, or because you leave society's choices to impact your own, and favor others' voices over your own.

III. Finding Clarity & Confidence

What is the solution, then? To summarize it in a single word: Awareness. Knowing that you can be influenced is a step toward self-discovery. Your life's journey is about engaging with life in such a way that resonates with the core of who you are. Embracing this complexity, striving to understand yourself better, and taking charge of your life are the fundamental concepts of a mindset that makes you bolder and more confident when making decisions. Wherever you are, or whatever you do, your nature as an intricate and fascinating social being is the essence of your human experience. All these facets contribute to the doubt you face in your decision, and acknowledging them empowers you to make choices that align with your true self.

Making the right decision is a deliberate process that requires self-awareness and authenticity, and should be balanced with a logical and scientific framework. Whether you are an artist seeking creative inspiration or a doctor deciding a patient's treatment plan, your decisions are shaped by who you are and the world around you. Authenticity, defined as the alignment of your actions with your core beliefs, plays a crucial part. Self-awareness and authenticity alone are not enough, though. Emotions and personal biases sway even the most authentic individuals, and that is where logical and scientific frameworks come into play. These frameworks, grounded in fact, logic, and reason, guide you to apply principles that transcend personal biases and preferences. The balance between the internal compass of authenticity and the external guidance of logic forms a robust decision-making process. And so, the marriage of inner awareness and scientific rationale enables you to make decisions that are both right for you and aligned with the broader context of your life. This way, you can choose a direction that is informed by both your heart and your head.

How do you go about solving this, then? How can you be in control of your brain to see things and eventually do things the way you want? The answer is simple: being equipped with the technical knowledge and the awareness of various decision-making frameworks and techniques, and becoming proactively aware of who you are and what you want before you are even placed into the response position of making a decision. This strategy empowers you to have the clarity and confidence needed to make the right decision, regardless of the pressure or uncertainty that comes along with it. Throughout this book, you will be presented with many logical and scientifically supported decision-making frameworks for each type of decision you make. You will find a detailed walkthrough on how each framework operates and how and when to utilize it. This way, you will have a reference to return to when you wish to take a logical and scientific approach to make your decisions.

You make around 35,000 decisions per day, 226.7 decisions just about food every day. that is a whole world of decisions right there on your dinner plate! My job throughout this book is to provide you with a practical playbook to help you both comprehend these decisions and find the clarity and confidence to make them right. In these pages, I will help you discover what is happening inside your head when you face a decision. Together, we will dive into cognitive dissonance and uncertainty-identity theories and see how they relate to you. As we explore further, I will introduce you to various terrains of decisions that are part of your daily life: personal, professional, relationships, careers, businesses, and finances. We'll examine real-life examples and case studies you can relate to and learn from.

This book is designed to take you through the natural decision-making process you automatically go through every day. It is not meant to be a theoretical "should do" formula but rather a practical reference you can always refer to whenever you feel stuck when making a decision. In the first part of the book, you will discover how your brain stimulates a decision-making process. You will be empowered by the knowledge and tools to take control of your perspectives, emotions, and the overall situation. You will be equipped with neuroscience knowledge, tools to differentiate between the decision types and the framework to use for each of them, a more emotionally intelligent approach to managing your initial emotions toward a decision, and -most importantly- the right mindset to embrace your responsibilities toward making this decision in a mentally healthy manner.

In the second and third parts of the book, you will go through all the techniques required for you to generate creative and empowering possibilities. Starting with the right strategies to gather information, going through what is considered reliable data and what is not, and landing at the tools to form different possibilities, all aiming to maximize the impact of your decision. You might probably find it to be the most exciting part because it will also take you through who you are and how to know what you want. I will introduce you to two of my dearest frameworks. The IVIC Decision-Making Framework© and The Authenticity Pyramid©.

To address the self-awareness side of things and to provide you with the clarity and confidence to know what you want, I am taking this book as an opportunity to present the IVIC Decision-Making Framework©. IVIC Decision-Making Framework© is a reliable tool that I have crafted after years of psychological research and coaching experience. I am sharing it with you to infuse your decision-making journey with clarity, authenticity, and confidence.

IVIC is the abbreviation of the four pillars upon which the framework was built:

1. Identity: Which choice expresses who I am?
2. Vision: Which choice do I want?
3. Impact: Which choice empowers me to make the biggest impact?
4. Cost: Which choice can I afford?

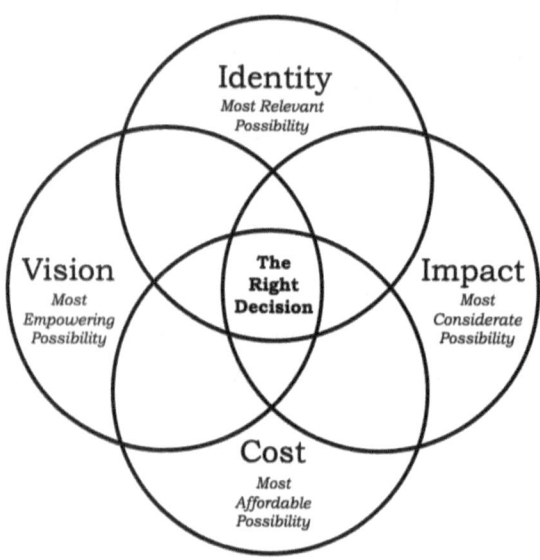

IVIC Decision-Making Framework©

The first pillar of this framework, Identity, is the foundation on which you construct your decisions. Rooted in the psychological theory of self-concept, it involves a deep dive into understanding who you truly are: your values, passions, talents and abilities, perspectives, and beliefs. I will also introduce another framework, Authenticity Pyramid©, to help you further explore your inner self and gain clarity on who you are. This clarity about your identity helps you to eliminate options that don't resonate with your authentic self, narrowing down the field and simplifying your choices. The second pillar, Vision, is your beacon in the fog of decision-making. Your vision reflects what you want to achieve in life and the path you have charted out to get there. The field of positive psychology emphasizes the importance of a meaningful life vision in promoting overall well-being and satisfaction. In decision-making, your vision acts as a reference point, helping you evaluate how each choice could aid or hinder your journey toward your goal. The third pillar, Impact, brings your attention to the potential effect of your choices. Here, the field of cognitive psychology comes into play, underscoring the importance of evaluating the possible outcomes of your choices. Since your decision is triggered by someone else's decision, your decision will be an input for someone else to make a decision. And so, as part of an ecosystem, you need to be aware of the consequences of your decisions and the impact they have on other people, and the nature you are part of. Last but not least, the Cost pillar encourages you to weigh the trade-offs associated with each decision. This step is rooted in economic and decision theory, and urges you to consider what you stand to lose or gain with each choice. When you contemplate these trade-offs, you cultivate a more holistic understanding of your options and their potential implications and become more considerate of their consequences.

The fourth and final part of the book equips you with the mindset and emotional tools to properly make your decision a reality. It further addresses confidence and resilience after making a decision, covering conflict resolution, doubts, and setting boundaries. And don't think for a moment that this experience is dry and academic. This reading experience is about empowerment. I will show you neuroscientific frameworks and emotional regulation techniques that you can apply right away. They're practical, engaging, and tailored to you. I want to take you through the process of gathering information, forming possibilities, aligning your decisions with your values, and committing to choices. We'll look at the scientific approaches, intuitive methods, and strategies about you in the real world. You will come across interesting stories, relevant case studies, and many exercises that will help you relate to the presented concepts and enable you to apply them immediately. With the insights and strategies laid out in this book, I will equip you to approach your decisions with greater clarity and conviction. Together, we will navigate the intricacies of decision-making across various domains of your life, translating complex theories into a pearl of actionable wisdom. This book is a pathway to empowerment, anchored in scientific understanding and further personalized for your unique life. Our exploration begins now, grounded in facts and guided by empathy. So, prepare to see your decisions and yourself in a whole new light.

Part 1 - The Stimulation Moment

"In the theater of existence, choosing to be an active participant rather than a passive observer is the first decision that shapes your reality."

Chapter 1

The First Impression

Dr. Paul Farmer co-founded Partners In Health (PIH) in the 1980s. As a physician and anthropologist, Farmer encountered devastating healthcare inequalities during his travels to Haiti. To him, the issues he saw were a call to action, and a decision point that would shape his entire life and contribute to global healthcare. The suffering, poverty, and severe access limitations to medical facilities he witnessed in Haiti were staggering. As opposed to feeling overwhelmed, Farmer determined opportunity and potential. The decision to establish PIH was subjected to meticulous consideration and in-depth analysis. It demanded weighing diversified criteria incorporating cultural references, available resources, potential partnerships, and an acute comprehension of the complex healthcare needs and medical care in impoverished communities as a whole.

This challenge was enormous and ought to be addressed. Many hold this viewpoint that providing high-quality healthcare in resource-poor settings executes an impossible task. Others argued that the primary focus should be directed toward more immediate, short-term solutions. Farmer's decision-making process, detailed in Tracy Kidder's book "Mountains Beyond Mountains" involved:

- Identifying the problem and weighing the ethical considerations
- Understanding the societal impact
- Generating alternatives
- Assessing the risks and benefits

PIH's approach was revolutionary in its simplicity and productivity. Farmer's decision to integrate community-based care with existing health systems proved to be a transformative model. PIH involved local communities, focused on prevention, and worked collaboratively with governments and other organizations, and that ended up with PIH significantly climbing one more step of the ladder in healthcare accessibility and high quality in some of the world's most underprivileged regions. Farmer's decision, rooted in a thorough understanding of the complex interplay between health, poverty, and social justice, constitutes a striking illustration of how recognizing and acknowledging a decision point can open doors to an impressive change. The story of Partners In Health demonstrates that decisions are not necessarily about opting between two clear-cut alternatives; sometimes, they involve unexpected pathways, challenging conventional prudence, and embracing innovative countermeasures.

How you are programmed

One of my clients, let us call him Bob, was significantly overweight. He was 173 cm tall and weighed 134 kg. Bob has lost his self-esteem because of how people would look at or deal with him. He avoided going on dates for years. Bob wanted to change his life and has worked incredibly hard for over 18 months to lose weight. He disciplined himself to stick to an intensive workout routine and a strict diet. Eighteen months later, we see a drastic turnover in Bob's life, successfully achieving a weight of 76 kg. He was in excellent condition; his body was lean, his fitness level was remarkably high, and his body shape was ideal, just like an athlete. This was not primarily the root cause of why Bob came to me, though. He contacted me because he was disappointed and depressed. After working so hard to be in a society-approved shape, people started commenting on his stretch marks. He could not hold back his tears while describing his story. I remember one prominent sentence he stated, "It is unbelievable. No matter how much I try, people always have sh*t to say!". Do you agree with Bob?

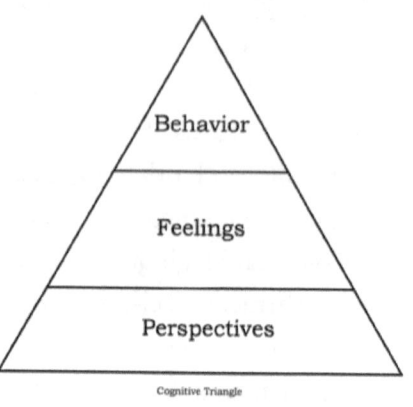

Cognitive Triangle

The initial inference when you face decisions may seem counterintuitive and might result in uncertainty. However, at the same time, it can potentially turn the tables and bring groundbreaking victories. Whether you are a teacher trying to encourage and uplift your students, an entrepreneur exploring a new market, or a parent navigating the challenges of raising children, you first need to define what these decisions mean to you. Society might not be your biggest fan, but you limit your potential to that of society's if you choose to follow the norm. As illustrated in the cognitive triangle, your behaviors are the products of your feelings, and your feelings are the products of your perspectives. So, if you wish to come up with better decisions (behavior) and accomplishments, you need to learn and figure out how to better feel about them. To do so, you need to have a bigger picture and perceive them in a more emboldening manner. For example, do you know why society deems it impolite to simply rest your elbows on the dining table? It is because, during medieval times in Europe, dining tables were often loaded with dozens of individuals sharing a meal. Placing elbows on the table consumed extra space, inflicting discomfort on fellow diners and potentially invading their personal area. Hence, refraining from resting forearms on the table became a symbol of respectable and ethical behavior and was further regarded as displaying "proper etiquette." Even in the present day, when there is typically enough space on the table for everyone, people still refrain from placing their forearms on it, although the issue of crowdedness no longer ceases to persist. I find it intriguing how we tend to follow conventions that omit logical reasoning and cohesive arguments, and only restrict our individual liberty to think and make decisions.

In 1966, Dr. Stephenson of the University of Wisconsin-Madison was as intrigued as I was about this phenomenon, and decided to conduct an experiment to further comprehend and gain insight into how it occurs. His attempt was to interpret, validate, and examine this contingency of society's prejudice and judgmental outlook. His objective was to unravel the enigmatic nature of conformity and the dominant influence of our ancestral traditions. At the very core of Dr. Stephenson's laboratory stood a spacious enclosure designed to house five inquisitive monkeys. Inside the enclosure, he placed a ladder leading to an enticing cluster of bananas suspended from the ceiling. The stage was set, and the monkeys were introduced to their new habitat. As the first monkey courageously ascended the ladder to reach the alluring bananas, Dr. Stephenson unleashed a deluge of cold water onto the climbing monkey and its companions. Soaked and incredibly stupefied, the monkeys retreated to the corners of the enclosure. The monkeys then executed periodic attempts to obtain their prize, only to be met with a frigid spray of icy water every single time. Eventually, they learned to avoid the ladder and keep away from it. The chilling consequences of their pursuit dampened their spirits.

Now comes the thrilling and most stimulating part of the experiment. Dr. Stephenson decided to introduce a new monkey into the enclosure. This newcomer, ignorant of the watery doom that had befallen its predecessors, eagerly approached the ladder to assert ownership of the bananas. But, before the new monkey could begin its ascent, the others pounced on it, dragging it away from the ladder and punishing it for its transgression. One after the other, Dr. Stephenson swapped the original monkeys with the newcomers, each experiencing and encountering similar results as the first. Soon, none of the original monkeys, who were being sprayed with icy water, remained in the cage, yet the new inhabitants continued to uphold the unspoken rule despite never having endured the icy punishments themselves. Bound by conformity, the monkeys perpetuated the cycle of punishment without identifying the underlying reason that lurks behind the curtains. The ladder and the bananas stood as an exemplary testament to the forceful unconscious influence of tradition and the weight of unchallenged customs.

Before you reflect on this story and start questioning everything you have encountered, allow me to acknowledge that doubt may not be a pleasant emotion. But, as Voltaire famously quotes, "Absolute certainty is absurd". In today's fast-paced world, certainty can swiftly alter and switch to the point that what was true in the morning can become utter gibberish by evening. Therefore, this book will challenge your standpoint if you firmly believe in uncontestable truths without any room for flexibility and adaptability. Only a valiant soldier dares to question against the odds and ideologies that define him. Honestly, it is imperative to do so if you want to make decisions that allow you to have the life you desire, and any form of dogma restricts your potential to reach greater altitudes. On the other hand, stepping into the unknown with an open, aware, and flexible mindset grants you the opportunity to explore the ever-evolving factual truths. You recognize that every detail you perceive is an opinion, and what you observe is a subjective assessment that can guide your decision-making process with more clarity and confidence. Even if you are basing your foundational views on factual evidence like I do, your belief will still be shaken by the same logic that anchored it in the first place. For example, over the past decade, 98% of knowledge about the human brain has been uncovered, and 80% of what was believed in 1990 has been disproven. This advancement proves that learning is bound to change, reshaping your meta-cognitive astuteness and their ever-evolving authenticities.

Consider a chef in South America experimenting with novel flavors, a young entrepreneur in Asia launching a startup, or an artist in the Middle East challenging traditional artistic styles. Each of these decisions, whether professionally or personally, expresses that individual's distinctive path. These choices shed light upon an open, excited, and determined mindset ready to welcome challenges confidently. Similarly, a European scientist discovering new methods or an African community leader promoting social change might face obstacles along the road. The main reason this happens is because people tend to stick to established practices, and if anyone challenges an unjustified tradition, they receive criticism or stand out isolated, different from the crowd. Even if it regards social issues, expressing opinions on controversial and hot-burning matters could result in severe judgment. Whether you advocate for environmental protection in a Western society or human rights in a conservative Eastern community, your stance might face opposition. I have personally met much criticism and have been labeled "insane" and "foolish" when I decided to turn down a good job opportunity and chose to spend 4 years volunteering with NGOs. If you are wondering what happened next, I ended up interacting with more than 20 different people across Africa and Asia, and the experience of blending with simple people to contribute in solving their problems has changed who I am forever. Staying in a 'stable job' would have never given me that much life experience and personal growth. Society gave me the same reaction a few months ago when I decided to leave my stable job and start my own solopreneurship career. In less than 3 months, I was able to double my monthly income, and -instead of holding one professional title- I found myself partnering up with six major governmental and private organizations on consulting and coaching projects. You see, if I have left my decisions for other people to make, I wouldn't have been here writing this book to you. Imagine what you can also do if you decided to break the queue and make your decisions the way *you* want to make them.

Here, the aim is to approach life through a different lens, and be ready to discover and smoke out the truth that fits you best. Trust me when I say that the most brilliant way of becoming confident and making decisions without hesitation is to embrace the decisions with authenticity and courage, knowing that what might seem assertive today may unfold tomorrow. I scribble down upon these words having in mind that you are a parent in North America deciding on educational paths for your children, a health worker in Europe adapting to new medical protocols, or a farmer in Asia implementing sustainable practices, and I have faith that your willingness to explore, question, and adjust does shape your unique journey. When you decide to be entwined with the ever-changing nature of truth and realize that certainty is not absolute, you navigate your route with a sense of empowerment and become guided by a consciousness that befits your own cultural, professional, and personal context.

I hear some pondering, "Much easier said than done!". You might be a CEO deciding to face the company's challenges head-on or a teenager tackling your complex society with determination. Whoever you are, whatever you do, life will present you with setbacks akin to a complicated childhood, rigid society, trauma, or health problems. Well, getting a handle on emotional or psychological challenges might be something you are facing due to factors outside your control, but blaming and victimizing won't get you anywhere. What makes a difference is how you respond to these challenges. Your decision to seek a helping hand, pursue therapy, or work toward recovery rests with you. Despite these challenges, you are responsible for playing your cards as well as you can. Are you sensing a shift in your perspective as you continue to read this? Becoming more aware of your thoughts and emotions, feeling more present? I wish!

So, how do you get a handle on these inner struggles, to make sure your mind is clear and able to make a good decision? Your mind's complexity is split into conscious and subconscious elements. Imagine a massive glacier with a 30-meter tip visible above the water (your conscious mind) while an enormous 3000-meter portion remains hidden beneath (your subconscious mind). This unseen part is your existence's engine room, controlling automatic functions like breathing, blood circulation, and digestion. The more aware you become of your subconscious mind's operation, the more control you gain, allowing you to break ingrained thinking patterns. In case you are wondering how present, conscious, and aware you really are, visit Exercise 1.1 in the Appendix section. It is a quick exercise specifically designed for you to explore whether you are truly present and aware of your thoughts, or leaving your brain to operate on autopilot.

How you operate

Your response to the argument in this chapter reveals who you are and how you approach challenges. Interestingly, your reaction may be guided by what we call a growth mindset. As coined by psychologist Carol Dweck at Stanford University, a growth mindset is the belief that your abilities and intelligence can be developed through hard work, dedication, and a love of learning. It is the idea that you can grow and adapt, and that failure is not a permanent state but a stepping stone toward success. Now, when you approach a challenging decision with a growth mindset, you see it as an exciting opportunity. You know it might be tough, but you also believe you can learn and grow from the experience. For instance, a study from the Harvard Business Review in 2012 highlighted that individuals with a growth mindset were more likely to embrace complex challenges, finding them as avenues for personal and professional development. Contrarily, if you approach that same decision with a fixed mindset, believing that your abilities are set in stone and unchangeable, you might see this challenge as a threat. This mindset is sabotaging, because it leads you to stress and anxiety as a response to the complexity that seems insurmountable without the belief that you can grow.

Your life is full of decisions, from minor to monumental, and understanding how you perceive these choices and learning to approach them with a growth mindset transforms how you make decisions. Whether you are facing a career move, financial choices, or personal relationships, a growth mindset is the key to unlocking a more fulfilling and adventurous life. To further understand this, I want to take you on a joyride through an extraordinary theme park that is your brain. Our spotlight will fall on the limbic system, a sophisticated network of structures with quirky personalities working in perfect harmony to make you. Now, what makes this journey even more exhilarating is understanding how this neural fiesta directly influences your everyday decisions.

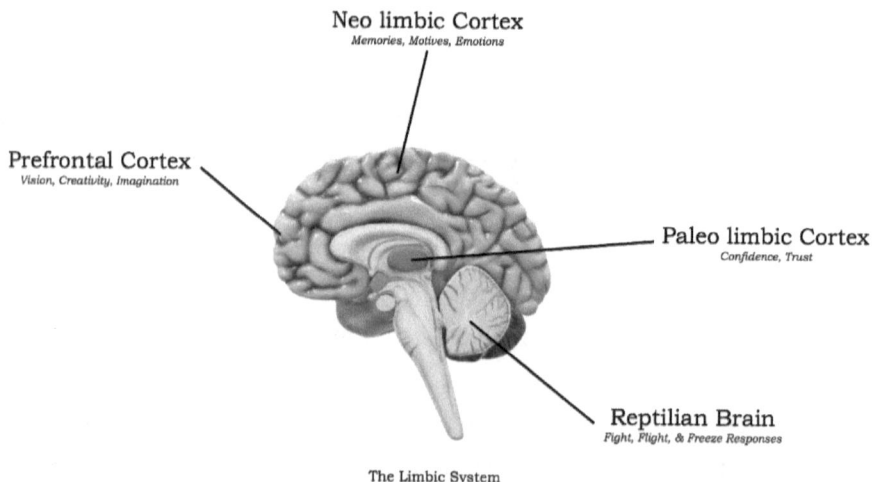

The Limbic System

We will begin our exploration with the stalwart guardian of your brain, the Reptilian Complex. Think of it as your brain's loyal watchman, always alert and ready to react at the slightest indication of threat. This ancient portion of your brain, ruling from the basement of our neural tower, is primarily in charge of your fight, flight or freeze responses. Remember when you nearly dropped your coffee cup, but your hand shot out just in time to catch it? that is your Reptilian brain springing into action. According to neuroscientists, around 80% of neurons involved in these reflexive survival responses are clustered in this area. Whenever you feel stressed, frozen, angry, or indecisive when making a decision, it might be because you perceive the consequences of this decision as a threat rather than an opportunity.

Just one floor up, we find the Paleo-limbic Cortex, the trustworthy diplomat of your brain. This area is your social compass, helping you cultivate trust and confidence in others. It is why you feel an instant connection with your best friend but remain wary of that suspicious character lurking in the shadows of a thriller movie. The Paleo-limbic Cortex provides the backdrop for your interpersonal interactions. This part of your brain is probably in charge if your decision-making's main driver is confidence or trust. For instance, if you hire a person to handle a task for you based on how much you trust them rather than how much they are actually capable of doing the job, it probably indicates that you are more driven by the sense of emotional safety over the practicality of achieving your goal.

Climb another level, and you'll step into your brain's bustling marketplace, the Neo-limbic Cortex. All of your memories, emotions, and motives find their home over here. When you catch the scent of a certain perfume and a wave of nostalgia hits, or when you feel an irresistible craving for that late-night ice cream, that is when the Neo-limbic Cortex is in action. Research from Nature Neuroscience shows that this region plays an indispensable role in generating emotional memories similar to those that occur spontaneously in our daily lives. Whenever you make a decision based on "What you know has worked/has not worked before," it means you depend more on referencing previously stored information and experiences rather than favoring the innovative possibilities.

Finally, let us ascend to the pinnacle, the penthouse suite or the Prefrontal Cortex. This is your brain's control tower, overseeing imagination, vision, and creativity. The time you envisioned yourself nailing that job interview or the picture-perfect holiday you daydreamed about during a dull meeting, all thanks to your Prefrontal Cortex. Johns Hopkins University neuroscientists discovered that this area is crucial for processing abstract thoughts and complex problem-solving. The Prefrontal Cortex is what differentiates us humans from any other living being. Because this part of our brain is relatively huge, we can create medicine and build civilizations. The more the Prefrontal Cortex takes an active role in your decision-making process, the more objective and empowering your perspective of that decision will be and the possibilities it brings along with it.

You might have already started realizing how all of this ties into decision-making. Every decision you make is a team effort between these areas. Your Reptilian Complex evaluates the survival risks, the Paleo-limbic Cortex handles social implications, the Neo-limbic Cortex weighs the emotional cost, and the Prefrontal Cortex imagines the possible outcomes. Every decision is a blend of instinct, social factors, emotions, and foresight. Getting a handle on this process means making more satisfying and empowering decisions. If your brain labels a potential decision as a 'risk,' chances are you will have defensive emotions about this decision, and therefore, you will feel negatively about it. But, if you teach your brain to consider every decision as an opportunity to achieve what you want, you will consequently and automatically feel more favorable about the decision you have to make. For the record, this is what we call a positive mindset.

A positive mindset is about a fundamental shift in your thought process and perspective. It is not just about thinking happy thoughts but about a deeper understanding and perspective shift that influences your actions, reactions, and overall approach to life. A positive mindset is about finding the silver lining in challenges, and viewing them as opportunities to learn and grow rather than the insurmountable barriers. The decision to embrace these difficulties with resilience, supported by the belief in your ability to overcome them, and the confidence that you will navigate through them and come out stronger on the other side, is a life decision that is capable of taking your potential to a whole new level. This state of mind is contagious! It influences not just your personal happiness and success but also has a profound impact on those around you.

How to manage your perspectives

The power to determine your future lies in your seemingly ordinary, day-to-day choices. It could be a decision to pursue further education, shift career paths, adopt a healthier lifestyle, or engage in introspection and personal growth activities. All these decisions, over time, play a part in shaping your future. Behavioral economist Dan Ariely's work underscores how these small decisions, which might seem insignificant in isolation, become incredibly potent when seen as part of a more extensive, cumulative process. You are indeed capable of shaping your own future. This might appear to be a daring claim, particularly considering life's uncertain nature. However, it is a logical assertion deeply anchored in the realms of psychology, neuroscience, and behavioral studies. Steering your destiny does not mean orchestrating every single life event. Instead, it hinges on your choices and actions in reaction to these events. Accepted and extensively studied by neuroscientists worldwide, neuroplasticity speaks to your brain's capacity to alter and adapt based on experiences, behaviors, and even thoughts. This implies that you have the power to modify your thought patterns, influencing your decision-making, behavior, and, ultimately, your destiny.

Even biology further justifies that you are in full control of who you are and, consequently, how your life turns out to be. I am referring to an

13

exciting and innovative domain known as Epigenetics. Epigenetics is a trailblazer in the world of science, dismantling antiquated narratives and bringing forth a novel understanding of our inherent dynamics. It traverses the landscapes beyond the simplistic alterations in your DNA sequences and opens your eyes to how your perceptions, molded by your experiences, significantly shape your emotional state. In my own life, I was surrounded by the profound influence of my family. Their beliefs and values painted my world in a single tone. But as I matured, my perspectives began to transform. They started to diverge from the norms I grew up with, and I decided to detach myself from these ingrained familial influences that were embedded in my mind. Yes, it was a challenging journey, but let me tell you, it has been the most liberating one. Today, I look at my past not with resentment but with gratitude, for it has led me to this newfound bliss and awareness.

The avant-garde leaders of epigenetics offer illuminating insights into the physical and emotional issues many of us grapple with. They share a striking revelation: Your life is not a predetermined path dictated by your genes or perceived genetic destiny. Instead, your thoughts and the environment that envelops you shape your physical and emotional health. Dr. Bruce Lipton, a renowned figure in this field, asserts that less than 5% of diseases result from genetic inheritance, contradicting the widespread fallacy that your health solely dictates your genes. Dr. Lipton's revolutionary work with stem cells debunked the oversimplified belief that your genes solely dictate your fate. His findings demonstrate that the environment, not just the genes, influences cellular behavior. The power lies in your thoughts and perceptions. When you decide to shift these, you hold the key to altering the course of your cellular destiny.

This revelation should be nothing short of a seismic shift in your life. It dismantles the belief that your health is a predetermined fact. Your beliefs sculpt your biology and influence your behavior, guiding your brain to align with these beliefs. Negative thoughts, when internalized, can manifest into corresponding outcomes. The society you live in often makes you believe that you are at the mercy of external factors and that you depend on doctors and medications. While medical help has its place, it is crucial to recognize your innate capacity for self-healing. The real change begins from within you rather than seeking solutions outside of yourself. The concept of neuroplasticity gifts you the power to overcome past limitations and reinvent your existence. Today, an increasing number of individuals are waking up to this potential, taking proactive measures to take the reins of their destinies. I am not trying to convince you with some hocus pocus or mambo jumbo kind of beliefs; I am trying to bring your attention to how much control you have over your mind and body in preparation for the upcoming argument in the next chapter about how much power and responsibility you actually have.

And so, to sum up the point I want to make in this chapter, I believe you are at a point in your life where the images, labels, and stories you have told yourself about who you are might be more constraining than you realize. You and I can make this complex journey personal and understandable, walking through it together in a way that resonates with you, regardless of your background or experiences. Think of yourself as a constantly evolving being. The standards or labels you have used to define yourself have become more like barriers, keeping you from fully embracing life. It may seem a bit unconventional, but there is a powerful truth here: Letting go of those rigid definitions of yourself opens up opportunities to act, fail, learn, and grow.

For example, if you are stuck in an unhealthy relationship, you might find the courage to leave if you stop defining yourself solely by that relationship. Do not get me wrong, this is not about denying your feelings or your history, but rather about recognizing that you are more than just a partner. If you are a student who feels trapped by your rebellious image, you might rediscover your passion for learning when you admit that maybe your rebellion is more about fear than true defiance. If you are a professional, like an insurance adjuster, tied to the status of your job, you might find the freedom to pursue your true passion in writing once you allow yourself to look beyond your current role. And here's where it gets fascinating: Your problems and fears aren't as exceptional as you might think. I do not mean this as a put-down; It is actually quite liberating when you think of it. The fear that your plane will crash, your ideas will be mocked, or you will be singled out in some way is often rooted in a subtle belief that you are unique in ways that are both positive and negative. But in reality, this is a form of self-centeredness that can hold you back.

I encourage you to envision yourself in simpler, more common terms. You are not just a genius or a victim, a success or a failure. You are a student, a friend, a creator, an entrepreneur. The more you define yourself in these ordinary terms, the less everything around you feel like a threat. It is a perspective that resonates with research in psychology, showing that people who view themselves in more flexible and multifaceted ways often experience better mental health and resilience. I hear you, and I agree that this process is not relatively easy. It might mean letting go of long-held beliefs about your unparalleled intelligence or beauty or shedding a sense of entitlement that the world owes you something special. It is akin to a form of recovery, where saying goodbye to these exaggerated self-perceptions might even bring withdrawal symptoms. But the freedom that comes with this shift in perspective is profound. Your growth journey is about embracing a more balanced, grounded sense of yourself, recognizing your commonality with others, and opening up to new possibilities. This way, you are gaining a richer, more flexible understanding of who you are. And in the end, you will likely find yourself more empowered, connected, and fully engaged with the life you are actually living. If this argument has provoked your thoughts, and you are keen to define yourself in a more mere and simple way, I suggest you visit Exercise 1.2 in the Appendix section.

Chapter 2

Defining Your Responsibility

After months of introspection and thoughtful discussions, my client Adam (not his real name) finally decided it was time to reach out to a coach, and that is when our paths crossed. We agreed to hold weekly one-on-one sessions that would soon bring about some remarkable revelations for Adam. At the outset of our coaching relationship, Adam opened up about his childhood and teenage years in different scenarios. Unlike therapy practice, which deep dives into the past, coaching typically focuses on the future. However, sometimes, reminiscences of the past can be illustrative and lend a better understanding of the present. As Adam recounted his formative years, it became clear to me that Adam had always felt an absence of clarity. He believed this was because he had always been instructed what to think and do without the freedom to form his own thoughts. What became crucial was to help Adam see that he had been driven by the idea of doing the *right* thing or, rather, by what he perceived others would think was right. Unconsciously, Adam had been led by the need to be the 'good son' and not to let his parents down and make them proud. He saw himself as a puppet of his parent's expectations, but in truth, he had been striving to fulfill these expectations to spare them any disappointment.

Understanding the connection between responsibility and fault is vital to making the daily decisions that shape your life. Fault looks back at past actions, while responsibility focuses on your present decisions and their future impact. For instance, in a professional setting, an architect who finds a flaw in a building's design does not focus on who made the mistake but, on the decisions, needed to correct it. Similarly, in a personal context, for a family discovering a leak in their roof, the responsibility lies deciding how to repair rather than assigning fault to the roof. This distinction permeates all aspects of life, influencing about 35,000 decisions you make daily (this number is probably accurate; many sources have confirmed it). If a sentence in this book does not resonate with you, I may be at fault as an author, but the decision to continue reading is yours as a reader. Even if others contribute to unhappy circumstances, like a young artist facing criticism or an elderly couple handling health issue, the final responsibility is their own. Responsibility drives actions, and only by accepting this reality can you attain the clarity, confidence, and certainty needed to lead an authentic and value-driven life. To better look at how all of this reflects on your own life and the way you perceive decisions, I have three brief stories to share.

The Passive King

Louis XVI ascended the throne in 1774 and faced a turbulent period in French history marked by financial crises and social unrest. As the country's economic problems escalated, Louis XVI struggled to address the issues and make necessary reforms effectively. Instead of taking decisive action and assuming responsibility for the state of the nation, he often displayed a passive and indecisive demeanor. Amid mounting public dissatisfaction, the French Revolution erupted in 1789, driven by widespread social inequality, political corruption, and economic hardships. The revolutionaries sought to overthrow the monarchy and establish a more equitable system of government. The revolution gained momentum, and Louis XVI and his wife, Marie Antoinette, became the symbolic figures of the monarchy's perceived oppression and decadence. However, rather than taking responsibility for the grievances of the

French people and engaging in constructive reforms, the king resorted to a victim mentality, believing he was powerless and subject to the whims of fate. Louis XVI's lack of personal responsibility and failure to adapt to the changing political landscape had severe consequences. In 1792, the monarchy was abolished, and France declared itself a republic. Louis XVI was eventually arrested, put on trial for treason, and found guilty. On January 21, 1793, Louis XVI was executed by guillotine, marking the culmination of his refusal to take responsibility and adapt to the changing circumstances. I hear you think, "The king is so passive; he should have done something!" And right, you are.

The Rescuing Father

A kind father always wanted to make sure his children were safe and happy. He never stopped thinking about their well-being and always aspired to ensure they had everything they needed. One day, as he arrived late from work, he entered his son's room to check on him. The son was sleeping, and the father noticed that the son had forgotten to put his mobile phone on charge, which means that he is likely to wake up to a dead phone in the morning. Because the father cares, he voluntarily plugged the son's mobile phone into the charger, kissed him on the forehead, and left. The same thing happened the following night, and again, the father plugged his son's phone to make sure he woke up the next day to a fully charged phone. The following night, the father arrived home exhausted and went straight to his room to get some rest. In the morning, the father was surprised by the son blaming him for not plugging in his phone. I hear you think, "The father is spoiling the son! The son should take care of himself!" And right, you are.

The Ungrateful Nation

If you have seen the movie, 'The Imitation Game', you probably remember this story. Alan Turing played a pivotal role during World War II in cracking the Enigma code, a sophisticated encryption system used by the Germans to communicate their military plans. Turing's work at Bletchley Park, along with a team of codebreakers significantly contributed to Allied efforts in deciphering encrypted messages, ultimately helping to shorten the war and save countless lives.

However, despite his exceptional contributions to the war effort, Turing faced persecution and condemnation due to his homosexuality. At that time, homosexuality was considered a criminal offense in the United Kingdom. In 1952, Turing was arrested and convicted of "gross indecency" for engaging in a same-sex relationship. Due to the conviction, Turing was subjected to chemical castration receiving hormonal treatments that had severe physical and psychological effects. Tragically, he died by suicide in 1954 at the age of 41. I hear you think, "How come society rewards someone who significantly contributes to humanity like that? This is unfair!" And right, you are.

The above three stories support this fundamental realization: You are individually responsible for everything in your life, regardless of external circumstances, and you can do literally whatever you wish to do. While you may not always have control over what happens to you, you always have control over how you interpret and respond to those events. Again, your life is all about how you respond to other people's and nature's decisions. And so, how your life turns out to be is still a manifestation of who you are and how you choose to respond to these stimuli. Coming up with excuses, trying to be other people's 'hero,' or judging others when you are not in an official position to do so are all symptoms of a dramatic mindset.

Taking Responsibility

A typical drama story will usually be about a person who needs to be saved, a hero who wants to save them, and a villain who is causing trouble. Although it is usually entertaining following such a story, living these characters in real life ends up with one being less proactive and responsible than they can actually be, which is what The Drama Triangle helps us understand.

The Drama Triangle, originally introduced by Stephen Karpman in the 1960s, presents a model of dysfunctional social interactions and depicts a power game involving three roles: Victim, Rescuer, and Persecutor. Each role represents a common and ineffective response to conflict. The participants in the Drama Triangle may switch roles

Persecutor
"I can make others do things"
"I'm better/more competent than others"
"If others did things my way, everything would be alright"

Rescuer
"Things will be alright if they let me do it for them"
"Others can't help themselves"
"Others need me to sort them out"

Victim
"I'm helpless"
"Life is hopeless"
"I can't do anything"

during a psychological game, and when one role changes, the other two roles follow suit. It is very likely that as a human being, you can identify with or be identified by others in all three roles in different scenarios.

Louis XVI, victims often see themselves as victimized, trapped, helpless, and hopeless. They believe they are at the mercy of life and resist taking responsibility for their circumstances. Victims view themselves as powerless or inadequate and place blame on Persecutors (the latter being individuals or circumstances), and focus on how they have been wronged. They constantly seek Rescuers to solve their problems. However, if

Victims remain in this disempowered stance, they hinder themselves from making decisions, solving problems, initiating change, and experiencing satisfaction or fulfillment.

Rescuers, on the other hand, consistently intervene on behalf of Victims, attempting to save them from the perceived harm. Like the father in the story, they feel guilty when witnessing others in trouble. Rescuers may have good intentions and strive to "help" others as they see fit. However, they fail to realize that by providing short-term solutions, they perpetuate dependency on Victims and neglect their own needs. As a result, Rescuers often find themselves overwhelmed, exhausted, and unable to complete their own tasks as they are constantly firefighting for the Victims. At the same time, Victims become more interdependent on the Rescuers, like how the son stopped taking responsibility for charging his own phone and started depending on his father to do it for him.

Persecutors resemble "Critical Parents" who adopt a strict and rigid approach, setting boundaries. They feel the need to win at any cost. Persecutors blame Victims and criticize the behavior of Rescuers without offering appropriate guidance, assistance, or solutions. They excel at finding faults, exert control through order and rigidity, and oppress the Victims. In some cases, perpetrators may exhibit bullying behaviors as well. In the Ungrateful Nation story, the United Kingdom as a nation forgot the historical role Turing played in weighing the war to their favor, and focused on condemning him instead.

Personally, this enlightening journey into the Drama Triangle compelled me to reevaluate my perceptions and aspirations. I broke free from the revolving roles and became the director of my own life. As a result, my attitude shifted, my belief system evolved, and my professional performance soared. My relationships blossomed, and I discovered a new wave of personal and professional success. My own journey of transformation taught me the invaluable lesson that the power to shape my life's trajectory rests squarely in my own hands, irrespective of the external scenery. This understanding, dear friend, is an awakening to the power of proactivity and a gateway to unimaginable professional and personal growth. Now that you are familiar with the Drama Triangle and the dynamics of roles within this triangular setting, let us consider your perceptions of life and, more importantly, your aspirations: Do you have the mindset of a victim, a rescuer, or a persecutor? If you are interested in figuring this out, please visit Exercise 2.1 in the Appendix Section.

Liberating Your Decision-Making Power

Beliefs separate us, and values unite us. And I would like to highlight that this chapter is about values and not beliefs. I deeply respect your personal beliefs, whether they are rooted in religion or personal worldview. I say this because we have now arrived at a juncture where we can engage in some hearty debate about responsibility as a value. However, if you are of the belief that life just happens to you, why are you still invested in this book anyway? If you believe that you do not have control over your life, it means you should not bother learning about how to make your own decisions, and let life do you anyways, and you could have set aside this book quite a while ago, right? So, I will assume that, since you are still here with me, you believe that you do hold the reins to your destiny and have control over the decisions you make and how they shape your life. This being said, let me tell you how a personal experience in Africa inspired me to write this chapter.

I was not acquainted with the Green Belt Movement until I visited Kenya in 2013. I was intrigued by a large street poster, and my local guide shared the tale of the woman in the picture, Wangari Muta Maathai. Born in 1940 in Nyeri, a rural region of Kenya, Maathai was fortunate to receive a quality education in an era when girls were not typically schooled. A scholarship took her to the United States for further studies, and she later became the first woman in East and Central Africa to earn a Ph.D. at the University of Nairobi. Upon her return to Kenya, Maathai was taken aback by the severe environmental degradation that had taken place during her absence.

Deforestation was rampant, biodiversity was plummeting, and the shortage of firewood and clean water was causing great hardship for many. Maathai took it upon herself to make a difference. In 1977, she established the Green Belt Movement, an environmental initiative concentrating on tree planting, conservation, and women's rights. The movement encouraged rural Kenyan women to plant trees, thereby fighting deforestation and concurrently improving living conditions with a reliable source of firewood and clean water. Despite facing considerable opposition, harassment, and even imprisonment for her activism, Maathai remained undeterred. The Green Belt Movement expanded beyond Kenya's borders to other African nations. By the time she passed away in 2011, the movement was credited with planting over 51 million trees, significantly improving the quality of life for many Kenyans and slowing down the deforestation rate. But perhaps even more impactful, Maathai's work catalyzed a major shift in mindset, placing environmental responsibility at the forefront in Kenya and throughout Africa. In 2004, she was honored with the Nobel Peace Prize for her contributions to sustainable development, democracy, and peace, becoming the first African woman to receive this prestigious award.

There are countless stories like Maathai's. When you look back at human history, it is clear that our world is a product of decisions made by people. Take this very book as an example. I decided to immerse myself in the experiences I had, and then dedicate time and effort to document them. The publisher decided to facilitate that this book reaches you, and you decided to purchase it and spare the time to read it. In this process, you, the publisher, and myself, have all made our own decisions. This sense of being in control of your destiny finds resonance in psychology, especially in the concept of the "locus of control." A study by psychologist Julian Rotter in 1966 differentiates between two types of control: internal and external. If you possess an internal locus of control, you believe that your actions and decisions can mold your life. In contrast, with an external locus, you are likely to ascribe your life circumstances to factors beyond your control. Research indicates that those with a strong internal locus of control often demonstrate superior stress management, heightened achievement motivation, and higher success levels.

Now, you might be questioning the unavoidable aspects of life, like the socio-economic status you were born into or the unforeseen occurrences such as accidents. Yes, these are undeniable truths, but your ability to shape your destiny stems from your response to these situations. Stanford psychologist Carol Dweck's research in 2006 on mindsets—your beliefs about your abilities and potential—backs this up. Dweck argues that those with a growth mindset view challenges and setbacks as learning and growth opportunities rather than conclusive assessments of their abilities. As explained in Chapter 1, this growth mindset allows you to confront difficulties with a sense of possibility, fostering resilience and tenacity—key components in driving your own destiny. At this point, I can recommend Exercise 2.2 in the Appendix section to reflect on your growth mindset.

Chapter 3

Managing Your Emotions

The Cuban Missile Crisis occurred in 1962. It was a 13-day confrontation between the United States and the Soviet Union initiated by the American discovery of Soviet ballistic missile deployment in Cuba. It is known as the closest the Cold War came to escalating into a full-scale nuclear war. During this high-stakes standoff, President John F. Kennedy had to make decisions of colossal consequence. One wrong move, and the world could have been thrust into a nuclear war. It is well-documented that Kennedy was initially furious upon learning about the missiles. He felt deceived by the Soviets, and his first emotional reaction was anger. But more importantly, he did not act on that emotion. The President's Advisory Committee, or ExComm, was assembled to handle the crisis. Their initial recommendations swayed toward aggressive actions like bombing strikes and a full-scale invasion. However, these suggestions were fueled by emotions such as fear and anger rather than rational thinking. Kennedy, acknowledging his own emotions and recognizing them in his advisors, decided to take a step back. He retreated to the White House swimming pool, a place where he could think.

This move was essentially Kennedy's attempt to control his emotional response, to step back from the emotional brink and gather his thoughts. He came back with a calm determination and steered the committee toward the decision to implement a naval blockade, a less aggressive move. His ability to recognize and manage his emotions and those of his advisors potentially saved the world from nuclear devastation. A study published in The Journal of Conflict Resolution in 2009 explored how Kennedy's emotional intelligence was key to this decision-making process. His capacity to control his emotions and not let them dictate his actions despite their intensity was instrumental in navigating this whole crisis.

See? Emotions, if unchecked, can lead to potentially disastrous decisions. However, they can also serve as insightful guideposts when recognized and managed. The goal, as Kennedy demonstrated, is not to suppress or ignore your emotions but to understand and navigate them effectively. Emotions are complex reactions to stimuli and thoughts, entwining physiological responses, feelings, and behavioral responses. Let us say you are confronted with a snake (the stimulus). Your heart races (physiological response), you feel fear (the feeling), and you might scream and run (behavioral response). That is an emotion at work. But then, what is the difference between emotions and feelings, you might ask?

Feelings are the conscious experience of emotional reactions. In other words, feelings are your personal interpretation of emotions. They are what you *feel* in your mind as a result of the emotion. While an emotion might trigger a physical response, feelings

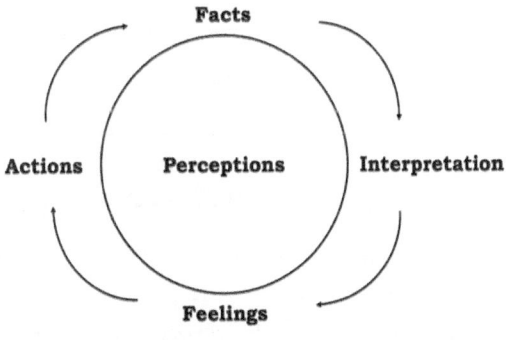

happen in the subjective world of your mind. Here is where it gets even more fascinating: The same emotion can lead to different feelings in different people, and the same person can have different feelings about the same emotion at different times.

For instance, pain is an emotion; the internal state you are in when being in an uncomfortable or undesirable situation (whether physically, or mentally). Suffering, on the other hand, is one possible feeling that could emerge as a reaction to pain. A good example is when you complete an intense workout at the gym. You are in pain, but not necessarily suffering. Although you could choose not to be in pain if you want to, you still understand the point of the pain you are experiencing, and therefore choose to embrace it rather than suffer because of it. Following the same lines, sadness is an emotion, despair or hopelessness are feelings that can result from prolonged or intense experiences of sadness, like during a period of grief. Surprise is an emotion, being startled or bewildered are feelings that can be reactions to something unexpected happening. Disgust is an emotion; the feeling of revulsion or repulsion arises as a response to something perceived as unpleasant or offensive. Anger is an emotion, feelings of resentment, rage, or irritation can emerge depending on the intensity and context of the anger. And so, when we talk about managing your emotions towards a decision, we actually mean being conscious of your emotional response, feelings, about this decision.

You see, emotions are a fundamental part of the human experience. They shape your interactions and responses and often add color to your daily life. Yet, when it comes to making decisions, unmanaged emotions -or better I say unmanaged feelings- act like a foggy window, obscuring the clarity and certainty needed to make well-informed choices. If you are an entrepreneur working tirelessly to build a business, excitement might take over when an unexpected opportunity arises. If this emotion guides your decision-making process, you might overlook potential risks, leading to a hasty investment that does not align with your business goals. If you are a parent who needs to make an educational choice for your child, your love and desire for their success may cloud your judgment and cause you to choose a school that looks impressive and prestigious but is not the best fit for your child's unique needs and talents.

Professional decisions across different fields and cultures share this theme. Whether you are a doctor making a critical medical decision or a young artist selecting a career path, emotions can divert you from a direction of clear, confident thinking. Emotions might pull you toward a familiar but less effective treatment or a creative pursuit that does not resonate with your true artistic vision. In relationships, too, emotions can be distracting. You may feel a strong connection with a friend and lend money without considering the potential strain on the relationship, or you might feel peer pressure to fit in and make choices that go against your values.

The key here is not to eliminate emotions but to recognize their influence on your decision-making process. The right way of dealing with emotions is to acknowledge them and seek to understand how they might be directing your decisions. This is how you cultivate a more balanced perspective. This balance fosters confidence and certainty in your decisions, helping you to navigate both professional and personal landscapes with insight and wisdom. Emotions are valuable, and they require careful handling when it comes to decision-making. This mindful attitude unlocks a level of clarity that supports your decision-making at all stages of life and in various contexts. It is about embracing a decision-making process that is confident, clear, and always rooted in the best interest of your goals and values. The more you understand your emotions about a decision and control how you interpret them, you become more in control of how you *feel* about the decision, and become more able to manage your emotions to become enablers rather than distractions.

Anxiety/Worry

First off, there are the classic anxiety or worry feelings. These twins frequently appear when you are anticipating a potentially negative outcome. As revealed in research by Kim et al. in 2011, your brain's amygdala, the key player in fear and anxiety, tends to overestimate risks in ambiguous situations, resulting in heightened anxiety. Your past experiences, more specifically the negative ones, might feed into this perception, inflating the threat level. Anxiety is a response to a potential, future, or uncertain threat. It is often associated with feelings of anticipation, worry, and unease. Imagine you are about to give a presentation in a week. Your mind may race with thoughts like, "What if I forget my lines?", "What if people judge me?" or "What if I mess up?". This is anxiety. It is tied to future events and possibilities and can linger over time, even when there is no apparent or immediate danger. At the heart of it, anxiety is a heightened state of arousal within you, a response mechanism intricately woven into your genetic code to perceive and react to threats. It is a relic from your ancestors, where rustling leaves could signal a predator. Even though today you are not typically encountering wild beasts, your brain still treats potential threats - like making a big decision - with the same fight-or-flight response.

Worry, the sibling of anxiety, is an intricate process where you continually contemplate potential issues or fret about the future. It is when your mind is on a constant replay, visualizing worst-case scenarios over and over. This process can keep anxiety levels elevated by ensuring that your focus is pinned on the potential problems, as suggested by Hirsch and Mathews in their 2012 study. Worry is not entirely detrimental, though. It is a way for your mind to engage in problem-solving, to predict and plan for potential hurdles. The problems arise when worry begins to dominate, leading to ongoing anxiety that can interfere with everyday life, including decisions you need to make.

Feeling anxiety and worry when facing decisions is mainly due to the uncertainty that comes with the outcomes. You might fear the wrong choice, regret missed opportunities, or be concerned about potential negative effects if things don't go as planned. This fear can be heightened if you have had negative experiences from past decisions, as your mind might predict similar outcomes subconsciously. And so, managing anxiety and worry is all about understanding that they are merely signals, not absolute predictors of your future. When you realize that these feelings stem from perception rather than reality, you are able to approach them with more objectivity.

It is entirely normal to find yourself tangled in the webs of anxiety or worry, especially when faced with a difficult decision. There is a potent cocktail of uncertainty, anticipation, and perceived high stakes that tends to brew anxiety. But let us flip the script for a moment, shall we? Exercise 3.1 in the Appendix section will help you further define where the anxiety and worry feelings come from, and how to take control over them.

Fear

Anxiety and worry could be forms of fear, but fear has a slightly different nature. Fear itself is an immediate response to a specific, identifiable, and real threat or danger. Let us say you are crossing a street, and a car ignores the traffic signal and races toward you. Your heart rate increases, your palms may sweat, and you instinctively jump back onto the sidewalk. This is fear. It is direct, immediate, and linked to a clear and present danger.

Fear typically arises when your brain perceives an immediate threat, either physical or psychological. If you have experienced painful consequences due to past decisions, this fear could intensify, causing you to avoid making similar decisions in the future. In the face of danger, your brain - specifically the amygdala, the center for emotional processing - triggers the release of hormones such as adrenaline. These hormones prompt physical changes like a faster heartbeat, quickened breathing, tense muscles, and sharpened senses. The immediate, potent reaction prepares your body to deal with the perceived threat. However, the complexity of fear lies in the fact that it is not always tied to an actual immediate danger. Fear can arise from anticipated threats based on your past experiences, learned behaviors, and personal perceptions. For instance, if you have a history of getting tongue-tied during public speaking, the mere thought of addressing an audience can trigger fear, even though there is no immediate physical threat involved. In this case, the fear originates from your memories of past experiences and your anticipation of negative outcomes.

So, how can you handle fear? Recognizing the source of your fear is the first step. Understanding why a situation scares you helps you reassess its threat level and formulate a plan to face it. There are several proven techniques to manage fear, from exposure therapy, where you gradually confront the source of your fear, to cognitive restructuring, which involves changing your thought patterns related to the fear, to relaxation techniques, which help mitigate the physical manifestations of fear. Exercise 3.2 in the Appendix section will help you navigate through your fear and take control over it.

Stress

Now, onto stress. Stress is a state of emotional strain when you feel overwhelmed by the demands of a situation. When you are undecided and the clock is ticking, or when the stakes are high and the decision you need to make puts too much at risk, stress could sneak in and cause psychological and physical discomfort. You have probably encountered stress quite a few times. You may have felt it seeping into your day at the office when deadlines are piling up or perhaps during a particularly chaotic morning at home. In simple terms, stress is your body's response to pressure from a certain situation or event. It is a physiological reaction that occurs when you perceive a threat or challenge. Think of it as your body's internal alarm system. When this alarm bell rings, it propels your body into 'fight or flight' mode. This reaction releases a rush of adrenaline and cortisol, stress hormones that prepare your body for action -

quickening your heart rate, accelerating your breathing, and tightening your muscles.

The triggers of stress, also known as stressors, range widely. They could be anything from an impending work presentation, a hefty credit card bill, or even just the hustle of daily life. And it is not just negative events that are stressful. Positive happenings like getting married, moving to a new house, or landing a promotion can also act as stressors. The thing is that stress, at its core, is not entirely a bad thing. It is an evolutionary adaptation that helped our ancestors survive. In the face of danger, the stress response gives you the push to confront or evade the threat. You can probably think of situations in your life when stress has provided the extra energy or focus you needed to get through. But, when you lose control of your internal alarm system and become unable to switch off, stress levels stay elevated far longer than is necessary for survival and might lead to chronic stress. That is when it starts to feel like you are in a never-ending loop of fight or flight. Prolonged periods of stress take a toll on your physical and mental health and contribute to problems like heart disease, depression, and a host of other health issues.

The point being, stress, in essence, is your body's automatic defense mechanism against threats or challenges. It can serve as a beneficial tool to navigate through certain situations, but it becomes problematic when it overstays its welcome. Hence, knowing how to manage stress effectively is one of the most crucial skills in modern life. After all, your well-being deserves to be more than just an afterthought in the busyness of your day-to-day life. You can use Exercise 3.3 in the Appendix section to navigate through stress and take control over it.

Anticipation/Excitement

This is a feeling that is tingling, vibrant, and often associated with positive experiences. Anticipation or excitement is a complex emotion tied to your hopes, dreams, and, sometimes, even your fears. If you are standing in line for a roller coaster ride, your heart might beat a little faster, your palms become a little sweaty, and there is this buzz in your belly like butterflies doing a cha-cha. That, right there, is the excitement felt when looking forward to the thrill of the ride. At the same time, though, there is a sliver of anxiety about the unexpected twists and turns. That combination of joyous expectation and mild apprehension forms the essence of anticipation. According to a study published in the Journal of Experimental Social Psychology in 2010, anticipation, especially when linked to positive events, leads to improved mood and increased happiness. It is not just about the event itself, but also the period leading up to it that is packed with potential for joy. Think about an upcoming vacation or a big celebration and notice how even thinking about it brings a smile to your face. That is the magic of anticipation.

Excitement is like anticipation's more exuberant cousin. It shares a positive outlook but with an added dose of energy. When you are excited, your brain releases a cocktail of chemicals, including dopamine, the neurotransmitter often associated with feelings of pleasure and satisfaction. It is your body's way of rewarding you for engaging in an activity it perceives as beneficial. Excitement and anticipation are natural emotions, and they play a vital role in driving you toward your goals and aspirations. They make the journey enjoyable, not just the destination. Is that always a relatively good decision-making driver, though? Well, remember the last time you were super excited about a new gadget or a fashionable piece of clothing that you ended up buying without a second thought? Or when the mere anticipation of a vacation made you overspend on the accessories you might not need? That is how excitement and anticipation can sometimes cloud your judgment and lead to impulsive decisions.

Again, there is absolutely nothing wrong with excitement and anticipation. They bring joy to your life and make you feel alive. But when it comes to decision-making, particularly important ones, you must balance these emotions with logic and reasoning. Excitement is the engine that drives you forward, and reasoning is the steering wheel that guides you in the right direction, and you need both to reach your destination. Excitement can make you overlook the details and the potential risks associated with your decisions. It is like viewing the world through rose-tinted glasses where everything looks wonderful, but it may not present a complete picture. That is when you need to invite your inner critic to join the conversation.

Like any other emotion, you always need to step back when you are about to make a decision, especially when you are feeling particularly excited. Similarly, anticipation, especially when linked to a future event or reward, can create a sense of urgency that may push you to decide hastily. Here again, it is important to slow down. I mean, life must have shown you already how good things take time, and hasty decisions often lead to hasty mistakes. Exercise 3.4 in the Appendix section will help you manage the anticipation and excitement emotions. The goal is not to eliminate excitement or anticipation but to harness them in a way that enhances rather than hinders your decision-making.

Confidence/Security

Feeling "confident" or "secure"? Then, you probably perceive the decision as within your abilities based on past successes or knowledge. You see a clear path forward and trust in your capacity to navigate it. Confidence and security - they feel good, don't they? They flood you with a sense of assurance, painting the future in strokes of success. It is like standing at the edge of a decision, knowing that the ground won't give way beneath you.

See, confidence and security are a bit like sugar. Just the right amount can be beneficial, even necessary. But too much? It can cloud your judgment, leading to overconfidence or a false sense of security. That is when the risks start to fade into the background, unnoticed. It is like walking into a situation with rose-tinted glasses, convinced you are immune to stumbling blocks. Where is the feeling coming from, I hear you ask? It is your brain rewarding you for past victories. Consider this to be the other side of the Anxiety/Worry coin. When you have succeeded in the past, your brain recognizes this pattern and boosts your confidence and security. After all, your brain is not always the best at differentiating between past situations and the current one. Every decision you make is unique, with its unique set of variables and outcomes. And so, while confidence and security can provide the courage to make a decision, you need to balance them with a healthy dose of reality checks and critical thinking. In other words, it is as important to maintain a level of humility and awareness as it is important to trust your abilities and experience. You want to be confident enough to take the leap yet grounded enough to foresee the challenges and possible outcomes objectively.

When you are just about to make a big decision and you feel that solid confidence, pause, take a step back, and examine your emotions. Is your confidence stemming from solid evidence and rational thinking, or is it simply a byproduct of past success? Exercise 3.5 is an excellent tool to guide you through this process.

Guilt/Regret

There is also the chance you might feel guilty or regretful. Guilt usually pops up when you feel your decision might hurt someone else or go against your moral compass. Regret, on the other hand, stems from past decisions where you felt you made the wrong choice. You are a human, not a robot. Emotions like guilt and regret aren't your enemies but a part of the unique emotional cocktail that makes you, well, you. Now, you might wonder, "Why on earth am I feeling guilty when all I am doing is just trying to make a decision for myself?" Here's why: Guilt often springs from a sense of responsibility or obligation. You feel like you *should* do something, and guilt sets in when your decision contradicts this *should*. In a way, your moral compass is telling you to reconsider your decision. But guilt can be misplaced, too. You might feel guilty for not living up to someone else's expectations or standards, and that is not fair to you.

Regret, on the other hand, usually pops up after you have made a decision. It is a feeling of wishing you had done something different. Maybe you feel regret because the outcome of your decision was not what you expected or hoped for. The thing about regret is that it is often based on hindsight, which, as they say, is 20/20. You did not have the awareness and experience you have now when you made this previous decision, so how would you have known what is the best path to take?

I hear you wondering why these two emotions, guilt and regret, are presented to you together, although they are different emotions. The answer is, as you have learned in the previous chapter, it all goes down to your sense of responsibility and how balanced that is. You might feel guilty because you think you are victimizing someone with your decision, or you might feel regret because you see yourself as a victim of your past choices. Recognizing these Drama Triangle roles is the first step toward managing guilt and regret. Just as important is developing a sense of compassion for yourself. Making decisions often involves uncertainty and risk, and it is okay to make mistakes. Guilt and regret are opportunities for learning and growth. Keep that in mind; chances are you will start reconciling with these past decisions. Again, you want to aim for a balanced emotional state when you are about to make a decision. A decision made in the absence of guilt or regret might lack moral consideration or learning from the past, and a decision overshadowed by guilt or regret might be overly cautious or rooted in fear. So, if you are experiencing guilt and/or regret while making a decision, you would want to navigate these emotions in a way that informs your decision-making without paralyzing it. Exercise 3.6 in the Appendix section will help you achieve this balance.

Relief

Ah, relief! That rush of joy and tranquility when a stressful situation is finally resolved or when a difficult decision is made. It is like a gust of fresh wind after a stormy night, isn't it? You might be wondering why on earth would I suggest that you control such a pleasurable emotion? Is it not a positive emotion to experience? Well, yes, experiencing relief is generally positive. However, it is your response to that relief where potential issues may arise. Think of it like this: Relief often comes after resolving a tension-filled situation, like finally making a tough decision you have been agonizing over for weeks. When that tension lifts, you might feel such a rush of relief that you can overlook essential post-decision steps or ignore potential ramifications that still need to be addressed.

Guess what? Even after a decision has been made and the tension is resolved, it is possible to find yourself stuck in one of the three Drama Triangle roles—Victim, or Rescuer, Persecutor. Let us say you have made a tough decision to cut ties with a friend because of a conflict you had with them. The immediate relief you feel could prevent you from seeing that you have slipped into the Victim role, feeling sorry for yourself rather than focusing on what you can do to ensure a healthier relationship. Your sought-after relief might end up with you disregarding better decisions. Also, do not forget the hindsight bias—that is when you look back at your decision and think, "Oh, I knew it was the right choice all along!". It can inflate your confidence and make you underestimate the complexity of future decisions. That is a relief sneaking up on you! The point here is not about denying yourself the joy of relief, but rather making sure that the feelings of relief do not blind you to the realities of your decision or lure you into a false sense of security. Acknowledge and savor the relief while keeping a clear and conscious mind for the steps that follow. The end of one decision could be the beginning of another journey, and you will want to navigate it with your full awareness and understanding. The objective of the following exercise is to help you acknowledge and enjoy the feeling of relief without losing sight of the bigger picture. Exercise 3.7 in the Appendix section will help you sail through the sea of relief.

Part 2 - The Clarity Moment

"It is clarity that arms the confident with the swiftness of decision, turning each crossroad into a mere stepping stone on the path to their desired destiny."

Chapter 4

Decision Making Models

Some people are quick to seek ready-made manuals and guides to solve the problems they face. I think it is smart to leverage other people's work, but only if the context is being considered. When it comes to decision-making, there is nothing like a one-size-fits-all framework for making decisions. Decision-making is an art that requires a unique approach for every context. Just like an artist who chooses different brushes for various strokes, you need to select the right method for the type of decision at hand. Each type of decision demands a unique blend of analysis, intuition, wisdom, and courage. In this chapter, and to avoid overwhelming you with all the different types of decisions, I have chosen the top four decision types that do require a careful decision-making process. Of course, the possibilities and situations life throw at us are limitless in variety, and this book is all about providing pragmatic solutions.

The first type of decisions we will go over are critical decisions that have remarkable consequences. For example, if you are a government leader facing an environmental policy change, you must consider the long-term effects on the economy and the environment. Making this decision requires extensive research, clarity in understanding the multiple factors involved, and confidence in a well-thought-out strategy. Your certainty in this decision will impact not just your administration but generations to come. Quick decisions, on the other hand, call for immediate action and a different approach. Think of a soccer coach who has to make a split-second decision to change the game plan. Here, time is of the essence, and relying on intuition and previous experience might be the key to success. These decisions might not carry the same weight as critical ones, but they require a keen sense of awareness and agility. Thirdly, crisis-management decisions often involve both time pressure and unforeseen circumstances, with a lot on the line. Imagine an emergency room where the doctor is confronted with a natural disaster like an earthquake. This situation demands immediate, effective action, where balancing expertise, resource management, and rapid response is vital. The certainty in such decisions can save lives and minimize suffering. Lastly, complex decisions, where too many factors need consideration, require a more intricate approach. An example might be a family deciding to migrate to a new country for better opportunities. This decision involves evaluating factors like legal requirements, cultural differences, economic prospects, and educational opportunities for children. It needs a clear understanding of multiple aspects, collaboration among family members, and confidence in the choice. Now the question is, how do we approach making each of these decisions?

For Critical Decisions

The Rational Decision-Making Model has made its mark even in global politics. A shining example is President John F. Kennedy's handling of the Cuban Missile Crisis in 1962. Facing the dire threat of nuclear war, Kennedy and his advisors meticulously applied a rational, step-by-step process to assess the situation. They defined the problem clearly: Soviet nuclear missiles were being installed in Cuba, within striking distance of the U.S. The team

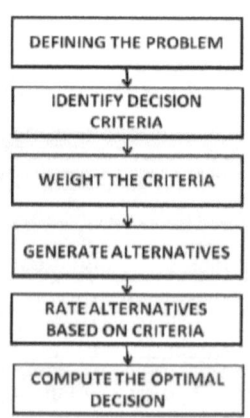

DEFINING THE PROBLEM

IDENTIFY DECISION CRITERIA

WEIGHT THE CRITERIA

GENERATE ALTERNATIVES

RATE ALTERNATIVES BASED ON CRITERIA

COMPUTE THE OPTIMAL DECISION

then identified and weighed various criteria like national security, international relations, and public perception. They generated alternatives, ranging from diplomatic negotiations to military strikes, and evaluated each against the identified criteria. After careful analysis, the decision to implement a naval blockade and pursue diplomatic negotiations with the Soviet Union was reached. This methodical approach helped avoid a potential nuclear catastrophe and led to a peaceful resolution of the crisis. Kennedy turned one of the most perilous moments in human history into a triumph of thoughtful and measured decision-making. Whether you are facing decisions in your personal life, professional career, or even navigating complex political landscapes, this model offers a proven path to sound and effective outcomes.

Perhaps you may be considering a career change, planning a major project, or choosing the right investment for your savings. The Rational Decision-Making Model offers a structured way to assess all the factors at play, ensuring that you are considering every angle and not just reacting on impulse. It is perfect for those complex decisions where you need to weigh various factors and want to ensure that emotions and biases don't cloud your judgment. On the other hand, for quick, intuitive decisions, this approach might be too cumbersome. Recognizing when to employ this thoughtful, systematic method is part of making it work for you, whether you are sending a rocket to the moon or navigating the equally complex realms of your personal or professional life. I have attached The Rational Decision-Making Model in the Appendix, Exercise 4.1.

For Quick Decisions

OBSERVE   ORIENT   DECIDE   ACT

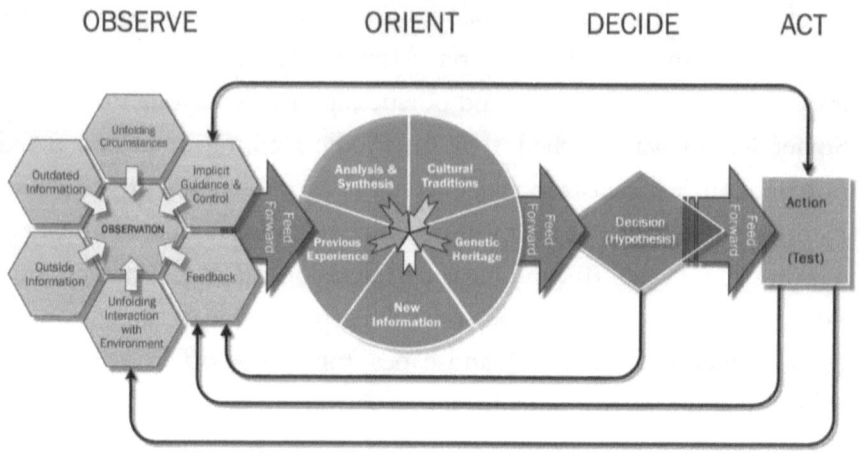

The OODA Loop (Observe, Orient, Decide, Act) has a rich history, particularly in military strategies. Its genesis can be traced back to Colonel John Boyd, a United States Air Force fighter pilot. Boyd developed this concept to train pilots to thrive in chaotic, rapidly changing environments. The Korean War is a classic example, where American pilots used the OODA Loop to maintain superiority in the air. By observing the situation and orienting themselves to the rapidly changing dynamics, they were able to make swift decisions and act with efficiency, often outmaneuvering their adversaries.

Let us translate that to your world. Say you are running a tech startup, and the market changes overnight. What do you do? You observe what is happening, orient yourself to the new reality, decide on a course of action, and then you act. That is the OODA Loop in action, a framework as fitting for the battlefield as for the boardroom. It is particularly useful when you are in a situation where things are moving quickly, and you need to adapt on the fly. But be mindful: It is not a one-size-fits-all solution. In decisions that need careful, thoughtful deliberation, the OODA Loop might leave you spinning. Knowing when to use this rapid-fire approach and when to slow down is the key to making it work for you. Whether it is on the sports field, in a bustling emergency room, or in a time-sensitive business deal, the OODA Loop is there to guide you when speed and adaptability are of the essence. Just like those pilots, you can dance through the chaos, turning confusion into opportunity. I have attached the OODA Loop worksheet in the Appendix, Exercise 4.2.

For Crisis-Management Decisions

Picture yourself in the control room of a major organization during a crisis. The stakes are high, and the situation is spiraling into chaos. This was the scenario facing IBM during the 2001 economic downturn. The company was wrestling with complex

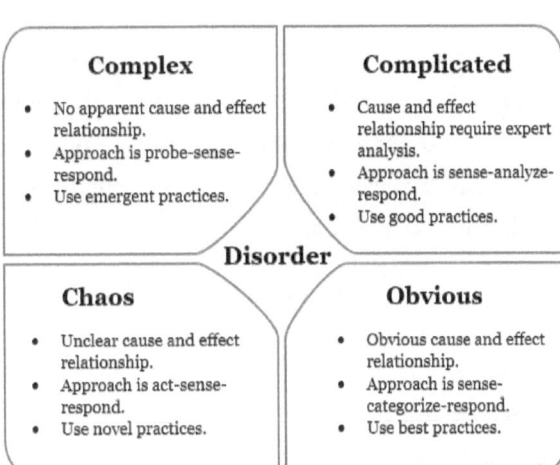

challenges in a rapidly changing environment. Here, the Cynefin framework played a key role in steering the company through turbulence by categorizing the challenges into distinct domains and tailoring strategies accordingly. This story illustrates the value of the Cynefin framework, not just in business but in diverse aspects of life where decision-making is pivotal.

Imagine you are an entrepreneur looking to break into an emerging market with a unique product. The market is unexplored, and you are uncertain how consumers will respond. This is where the Cynefin framework's complex domain comes into play. It is like navigating a dense jungle where paths are hidden, and each step may lead to surprising discoveries. In such cases, you need to probe, sense, and respond. Small experiments, like launching pilot versions of your product, can help you gauge the market response. This model is beneficial for innovators, researchers, or anyone stepping into the unknown, where cause and effect are only coherent in retrospect.

Now, consider a seasoned architect who's handed a project to build a sustainable skyscraper. This falls into Cynefin's complicated domain. The problems are multifaceted but not insurmountable. Experts can analyze the situation and find solutions. Just like solving a mathematical equation, the answer is not immediate, but with the right expertise, you can figure it out. If you are an engineer, a surgeon planning a complex operation, or a financial analyst weighing investment options, this domain helps you break down the problem, analyze the parts, and find the right solution.

In the middle of a natural disaster, such as an earthquake or a flood, time is of the essence, and decisions must be made quickly. This scenario fits into the chaos domain of the Cynefin framework. Here, cause and effect are unclear, and rapid action is vital. If you are an emergency responder or a pilot dealing with sudden engine failure, the chaos domain instructs you to act immediately, sense the reaction, and respond accordingly. It is akin to a medical emergency where immediate intervention can save a life.

Finally, in the obvious domain, things are clear and straightforward. Imagine driving on a well-marked road with clear signs and directions. That is the obvious domain. For IBM, this might have been routine operational decisions, like managing daily workflows. In this domain, the Cynefin framework advises you to sense, categorize, and then respond. You identify the situation, apply the best practice, and move forward. It is like following a tried-and-true recipe. This approach is widely applicable in areas like administration, standard manufacturing processes, or any situation where the path is well-trodden.

What makes the Cynefin framework universally appealing is its adaptability. It does not matter if you are a general on the battlefield, a startup founder exploring new horizons, a doctor facing medical complexities, or a homemaker deciding the best school for your child. The framework equips you to navigate diverse terrains of decision-making. From the individual's everyday choices to monumental decisions in history, the Cynefin framework serves as an insightful guide. This versatility makes it an indispensable tool, whether you are steering a corporation through an economic downturn, like IBM in 2001, or simply choosing the right career path. The Cynefin framework acts as both a compass and map, tailored to various landscapes and personal scenarios. It is not a one-size-fits-all solution but a nuanced, multifaceted guide that adapts to your unique situation. I have attached the Cynefin framework worksheet for you in the Appendix, Exercise 4.3.

For Complex Decisions

In the early days of Microsoft, a young and ambitious Bill Gates was looking to grow his company but was faced with a multitude of challenges and limited resources. It was during this crucial period that he stumbled upon the Pareto Principle or the 80/20 Rule. By 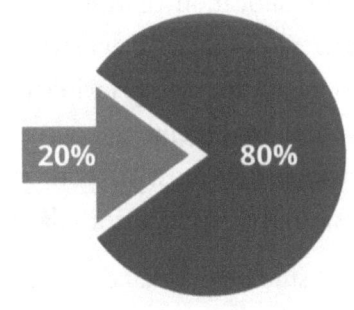 applying this rule, he was able to identify that a significant portion of Microsoft's revenue was coming from a few key products. Rather than spreading efforts thin across many projects, he decided to focus his energy on those few vital products that were delivering results. That decision proved pivotal for Microsoft and allowed it to grow and expand into the tech giant we know today. The Pareto Analysis or 80/20 Rule is a decision-making framework that essentially tells you that 80% of the results often come from 20% of the efforts. Named after the Italian economist Vilfredo Pareto, who initially observed that 20% of the pea pods in his garden produced 80% of the peas, this principle has found applications in diverse fields, from economics to personal development.

Suppose you are an entrepreneur trying to scale your startup. With numerous tasks demanding your attention, it is easy to get overwhelmed. Pareto Analysis encourages you to identify the vital few tasks or products that will bring the most impact. Focus on enhancing those, and you'll likely see a substantial improvement in your overall business without running yourself ragged. If you are a teacher planning a curriculum, identifying which 20% of the topics or methods contribute to 80% of student learning can significantly enhance your teaching effectiveness. Concentrating on those essential areas ensures that your students grasp the core concepts, even within a tight schedule. During a crisis, like a natural disaster, humanitarian organizations can apply Pareto Analysis to figure out where their efforts would be most effective. Recognizing that a specific allocation of resources can lead to the majority of the desired impact allows them to act swiftly and efficiently, even amidst chaos. Even in your daily life, this principle has value. For example, if you are struggling with time management, you may find that a small portion of your tasks contributes to most of your productive outcomes. Focusing on those tasks can free up time for relaxation or pursuing hobbies.

A study conducted by Richard Koch in his book "The 80/20 Principle" substantiates the widespread application of Pareto Analysis in business, personal life, and societal planning. So, whether you are a government leader aiming to improve public services, a parent trying to balance work and family, or a student striving to excel in your studies, Pareto Analysis offers a lens through which you can see what truly matters. It is not a strict mathematical formula but rather a guideline that prompts you to think about where your efforts will be most rewarded.

From the bustling tech hubs of Silicon Valley to the serene landscapes of rural villages for young entrepreneurs, seasoned professionals, or even retirees planning their life's next phase, the Pareto Principle resonates. It is about recognizing that not all efforts are created equal, understanding where your energy should be directed, and making decisions that align with your goals and values. It is a tool for the wise, a principle for the pragmatic, and a philosophy for those who seek to live life with purpose and efficiency. I have attached the Pareto Analysis Framework Worksheet in the Appendix, Exercise 4.4. Here is a brief guide to help you decide which framework fits your context the most.

Use Cases Examples	Framework	When to Use	How It Works
Launching a new product	Rational Decision-Making Model	Clear objectives, well-defined problem, time for analysis	Define the problem, identify alternatives, weigh criteria, evaluate alternatives, select the best option
Military strategies, emergency medical decisions	OODA Loop	Rapidly changing environments, quick decisions needed	Continuously cycle through observing the situation, orienting, deciding, and acting
Organizational merger, natural disaster response	Cynefin Framework	Various complexities, from obvious to chaotic situations	Categorizes problems into Obvious, Complicated, Complex, Chaotic; approach varies depending on category
Sales strategies, environmental efforts	Pareto Analysis/80/20 Rule	Identify major effects from minority causes	Determine key factors, measure effect, concentrate on 20% delivering 80% results
Crisis management in a corporation, on-the-spot decisions in sports	OODA Loop	Fast-paced, high-pressure situations	Quick and adaptive decision-making through continuous observation and action
Navigating political landscape, developing new technology	Cynefin Framework	Complex and uncertain scenarios	Understand the context and complexity; approach strategically with insights tailored to the situation
Buying a family car, planning a holiday	Rational Decision-Making Model	Decisions with many available options, time to consider	Methodically evaluate all options based on criteria such as cost, safety, preferences
Managing personal finance, prioritizing health goals	Pareto Analysis/80/20 Rule	Focus on the most impactful areas for personal improvement	Identify where small changes can make a significant difference, such as cutting 20% of spending that accounts for 80% of expenses

Chapter 5

The Power of Information

The year is 1984, and we find ourselves in the middle of a fierce battle between two giants in the soft drink industry: Coca-Cola and Pepsi. This battle, often referred to as the "Cola Wars," was about market share, brand loyalty, and winning consumers' hearts and taste buds worldwide. Coca-Cola, a brand with a century-old recipe considered sacrosanct by many, faced a significant challenge as Pepsi was steadily gaining ground. Marketing campaigns were making inroads, and taste tests showed that consumers preferred Pepsi's sweeter taste.

What was Coca-Cola to do? Their decision-making process led them to one of the most controversial moves in the history of marketing: The New Coke. Coca-Cola's executives embarked on a massive information-gathering campaign. They conducted blind taste tests with over 200,000 consumers. They poured resources into market research, studying consumer preferences and trends in sweetness in other food products. The data seemed clear: people preferred a sweeter cola. And so, they made a decision. They would reformulate Coca-Cola to be sweeter and more aligned with the modern palate. Being backed by data and extensive research gave them confidence that this was the right decision to make. But when New Coke was launched, it sparked an uproar that no amount of research had predicted. Letters flooded the Coca-Cola headquarters, protests were organized, and loyal customers felt betrayed. It was a public relations disaster. Why? What went wrong with all that information? It

51

turned out that while they had gathered extensive data on taste preferences, they had neglected to factor in the deep emotional connection that consumers had with the original Coca-Cola. Their information gathering had missed an essential human element, and the result was a decision that was logical on paper but failed to resonate with the hearts of their customers. Within a few months, Coca-Cola announced the return of the original formula, now branded as Coca-Cola Classic. New Coke lingered on for a while but eventually disappeared. Coca-Cola's executive team failed to realize the complex relationship between data and human emotion, and between numbers and nostalgia. Charts, graphs, and taste tests were not the *relevant* information to gather. Understanding people, their memories, their values, and their connections to a product or a decision were the factors that mattered. In your own life, whether you are making a personal choice or a professional one, gathering information is not a merely quantitative exercise. You need to delve into the qualitative aspects, understanding emotions, perceptions, and the intangible elements which guide you to a decision that resonates with you and those who will be impacted by it.

To differentiate between relevant and irrelevant information, you first need to learn how you, as a human being, process the information. It is similar to the way computers work. You take in information, process it, and then respond to it. This mechanism, which we call Information Processing Theory, is divided into three core stages: sensory memory, working memory, and long-term memory. The words you read on this page enter your sensory memory through your eyes, where they are held briefly before moving into your working memory. This is the part of your mind where the real action happens. You make sense of the words, link them with prior knowledge stored in your long-term memory, and suddenly, you have understood my message. Following the same process, when you need to decide on something, you gather information, process it using your working memory, and draw on your past experiences and knowledge stored in your long-term memory. And so, the way you make sense of information is basically dependent on how much sense *you* make out of it.

Question: Does gathering more information ensure making better decisions? Well, navigating the complex world of information gathering can feel like steering a ship through foggy waters. You know you need to get to the other side, but how do you avoid the pitfalls of having either too little or too much information? Let us explore this together, using a framework that might just become your compass. Picture yourself as Sherlock Holmes, trying to solve a mystery. Your task is to make a critical decision on the person guilty of a crime, and you need the right clues to do so. Your job is not to gather as much information as possible, but to gather the *right* clues. To do so, you need to start by defining what you are trying to achieve, or the key question you want to answer. It is like setting the destination for your journey; you need to know where you are going to understand the path you need to take. Next, you need to identify the criteria that matter most. Think about what is *relevant* to your decision. It is akin to choosing the right tools for a job. For example, if you are deciding on a new career path, consider factors important to you like potential earnings, work-life balance, and opportunities for growth. These become your guiding stars. Now comes the exciting part: gathering the information. If you are making a personal decision like choosing a school for your children, you would want to talk to other parents, visit schools, research online, and perhaps even consult educational experts. If you are a business leader deciding on a new market to enter, you will delve into market research, competitor analysis, customer feedback, and legal regulations. It is like gathering ingredients for a recipe; each one is essential to the final dish.

But how do you avoid the traps of too little or too much information? The answer lies in balance and relevance. You must ensure that your information is balanced, meaning you are not relying too heavily on one source or perspective. Pulling from different sources prevent biases and give you a more comprehensive view. Too much information, on the other hand, can be overwhelming. It is like having a library of books when you only need one chapter. The key is to filter your information through your guiding stars and the criteria you have set. Ask yourself: What is relevant? What is essential? What is noise? This filtering helps you focus on what truly matters. Credibility is another cornerstone of this process. Every piece of information should be examined with a critical eye. Who is saying it? What is their agenda? Where did it come from?

A fact from a renowned research institution or a reputable news source carries more weight than a random blog post or a hearsay opinion. In other words, the quality of the information you gather is as important as the quantity of it. This information-gathering process is a mindful, engaged, and responsive way to decision-making. It is about asking the right questions, seeking diverse perspectives, balancing your sources, and filtering through the noise. Exercise 5.1 in the Appendix section is an excellent guide to help you decide how much information is sufficient for a decision you want to make.

Collecting relevant information

And so, you stand at the crossroads of information, a vast landscape stretching out in front of you. On one side lies the path of wisdom; marked by technology, mentorship, coaching, and credibly produced content. On the other side, the path of misguidance awaits; littered with rumors, friends' opinions, unverified social media claims, non-credible published work online, and bias. Your journey depends on the path you choose, and the relevance and credibility of the information upon which you make your decisions are crucial for the quality of these decisions. Below is a detailed discussion covering the main information sources, and

I have also included Exercise 5.2 in the Appendix section to guide you through filtering the information sources.

Technology

AI, Big Data, and advanced analytics offer an unprecedented opportunity to gather insights. These can be your allies and the modern navigators guiding you through the dense fog of information. Platforms like IBM's Watson and ChatGPT provide information at a speed and accuracy that human minds cannot match. A report by Accenture reveals that 79% of executives believe that AI will help accelerate technology adoption throughout their organizations, amplifying the human experience. There are patterns hidden in those numbers, trends buried under layers of information, and answers concealed in the chaos of variables. This is where AI shines. It sifts through this complexity, finding the pearls of wisdom you need. From social media trends to stock market fluctuations, from weather patterns to healthcare statistics, Big Data binds it all into a coherent whole. It brings the world to your fingertips, allowing you to see global trends, local nuances, and everything in between. This panoramic view fosters empathy, understanding, and wisdom, transforming you from a mere observer to a global citizen. Advanced analytics is where science meets art. It is a dance of algorithms and creativity, where numbers turn into insights, where data sings a melody of meaning. Advanced analytics take the raw, unprocessed information and refine it, analyze it, and present it in a way that speaks to you.

You do not have to be a CEO or a tech-savvy expert to leverage the wonders of technology for personal decisions. In fact, in your day-to-day life, the power of technology is quietly transforming the way you think, act, and decide. It is a silent revolution that is democratizing access to insights, understanding, and wisdom, not just for big corporations but for you in your personal life. Consider the daily choices you make, from buying a new smartphone to choosing the right diet or finding the perfect vacation spot. Technology curates experiences, tailors recommendations, and builds connections that are uniquely yours. Platforms like Amazon, for example, leverage AI algorithms to analyze your purchasing behavior and offer personalized suggestions. These platforms understand you, your preferences, and your lifestyle, and guide you to make decisions that align with your behavioral trends. If you are planning a trip to a new city, then you probably realize that gone are the days when you had to rely on static brochures or one-size-fits-all travel guides. Smart applications like Airbnb use data analytics to offer localized experiences and connect you with local hosts, authentic cuisines, hidden trails, and experiences that resonate with your curiosity and adventure. Think about health and wellness as another area where personal decisions carry profound significance. Wearable devices like Fitbit, backed by advanced analytics, understand your body, your habits, your strengths, and your areas of improvement. They have become like personal fitness coaches who guide you toward a healthier, happier you. A study from Stanford University shows that wearables have the potential to detect illnesses such as Lyme disease and diabetes even before symptoms appear. This technology establishes an ongoing dialogue with your body and empowers you to make informed decisions that nurture and nourish your well-being.

Shift gears and take the realm of personal finance. FinTech apps like Mint or Robinhood simplify the complexities of budgeting, investing, and financial planning. They can become your personal financial advisors who demystify the jargons, break down the barriers, and guide you to make decisions that secure your financial future. The global FinTech market was valued at around $127.66 billion in 2018 and is expected to grow to $309.98 billion at an annual growth rate of 24.8% through 2022, according to The Business Research Company. This is a testament to how technology is making financial literacy accessible, practical, and tailored to your unique financial goals.

You see, technology in your personal life is enriching, engaging, and empowering, and can help you transform mundane decisions into mindful choices only if you stay in control of it. At the end of the day, this book's main argument is about you taking control of your life. And so, my advice to leverage technology to gather more insights and get more clarity is by no means an invitation to live dependently on it. Make decisions that resonate with your heart, align with your mind, and reflect your unique place in the world, and you can leverage technology to gather enough information and make wiser decisions. It is a dance with technology, where you lead, and technology follows, creating a harmony that is as beautiful as it is insightful.

Mentorship/Coaching

I am not sure if you already know this, but Steve Jobs mentored Mark Zuckerberg, Maya Angelou mentored Oprah Winfrey, Warren Buffet mentored Bill Gates, Mahatma Gandhi mentored Nelson Mandela, and Audrey Hepburn mentored Elizabeth Taylor, and the list goes on. What does mentorship mean to you in your personal and professional life? How does it transcend the confines of a boardroom or classroom to become a lifelong partnership, and a companionship that guides you, inspires you, and helps you discover the best within yourself? Technology, as powerful as it is, will never replace this human touch. The algorithms can analyze, predict, and even recommend, but they cannot *feel*; they cannot understand the subtleties, the emotions, and the very humanness of your decisions. That is where mentors and coaches shine. They blend the art of empathy with the science of experience, not by rules or formulas but by the nuanced, delicate, and profound understanding of what it means to be you in a world that is as beautiful and complex as the decisions you make. Whether in your career, your relationships, your future dreams, or your present day-to-day life, mentorship and coaching are two powerful sources of gaining enough wisdom to make the right decision.

What makes it so is that mentors and coaches challenge you, push you beyond your comfort zone, and provoke your thinking to navigate the complex, often confusing world of professional growth. Professional mentors and coaches are trained to be aware of your unique talents, your passions, and your aspirations, and know how to align them with opportunities that resonate with who you are. A mentor or a coach is a guide who has been where you are, felt what you feel, and emerged wiser and stronger. Think about those big life decisions, like buying a house, starting a family, or relocating to a new country. It can get overwhelming, right? The sheer volume of information, choices, risks, and uncertainties can leave you lost, anxious, and even paralyzed. That is where mentors and coaches step in, not with generic advice or textbook answers but with empathy, insight, and the gentle assurance that they get you. They have been there. They have felt the excitement, the fear, the doubt, and they have found a way through it. The wisdom they offer you is a personalized roadmap crafted from their experiences and your passion to grow. I, along with thousands of other coaches and mentors around the world, are here for you, and are waiting for you to make the decision and partner with us to gain the clarity and confidence you need.

Credible Published Content

Credibly produced content refers to peer-reviewed articles, well-researched books, and speeches by thought leaders who have devoted their lives to learning about their domains. When you navigate these waters, you are in the company of giants and guided by the best minds in the field. In your professional life, this challenge is even more acute. The stakes are higher, the decisions more complex, and the consequences more profound. Whether you are an entrepreneur seeking to disrupt the market, a manager aiming to lead your team to success, or an employee aspiring to excel in your role, you are faced every day with decisions that require insight, judgment, and wisdom. Where do you find this wisdom?

You find it in the scientifically validated research, and the expert opinions that stand tall, unswayed by trends, and uncorrupted by biases. Knowledge distilled from years of study, experimentation, and reflection is what I call credible content.

In your personal life, too, this commitment to credibility is vital. Think of the decisions that shape your life: the foods you eat, the exercises you choose, the places you travel, and the relationships you nurture. These decisions are the expressions of who you are, and they deserve nothing but the best, the most authentic, the most trustworthy sources of wisdom. Whether it is a diet plan backed by scientific research, a travel guide written by local experts, or a parenting book penned by renowned psychologists, this is about respecting yourself enough to seek the best, learn from the best, and be guided by the best. We will get deeper into this when we reach the Authenticity Pyramid© in Part III of this book.

Rumors

Nathan Mayer Rothschild, a key figure in the London branch of the family, was known for his intelligence and shrewd investment strategies. During the Napoleonic Wars, he had a network of agents spread across Europe, providing him with crucial information long before his competitors. The story goes that after the Battle of Waterloo in 1815, where the British and Prussian forces defeated Napoleon, Rothschild received the news of Wellington's victory a full day ahead of the government's official channels. This was because of his swift couriers and well-placed informants.

The rumor part of the story is where details get murky. According to some versions of the tale, Rothschild used his early knowledge to deceive the London Stock Exchange. He was seen selling British government bonds, leading others to believe that he had inside information that Britain had lost the battle. Panicked by Rothschild's actions, other investors began to sell their bonds, causing prices to plummet. Once the prices had fallen, Rothschild is said to have secretly bought up a large quantity of the bonds at a fraction of their original value. When official news of Wellington's victory arrived, and the markets realized that Britain had indeed won, bond prices soared. Rothschild's earlier purchases then allegedly made him a fortune. Too bad for those who sold their bonds because of untrusted news!

However, recent historical examinations have challenged the accuracy of this dramatic tale. Some historians argue that while the Rothschilds did profit from their early information, there is little solid evidence to support the idea that Nathan Rothschild engaged in a deliberate deception of the market. Moreover, the gains made after the Battle of Waterloo were likely just one part of the broader and more complex financial strategies that built the Rothschild fortune. The story of Rothschild's rumored deception has taken on a life of its own, symbolizing for some the cunning and secret maneuvering often associated with high finance. It is an engaging tale that captures the imagination, but it should be treated with caution as a historical fact.

Now, get this: I was researching to bring you a story about rumors and found this story, and I deepened my research to find that this story in itself might be a rumor! Got my point? To depend on rumors is like building a house on sand. It may look appealing at first, but it lacks the solid foundation you need. This house built on sand might be your career, your health, or your relationships. Whether it is a business strategy you are crafting, a medical treatment you are considering, or a financial investment you are contemplating, the foundation *does* matter. Building on hearsay or unverified information is risky and, may I even say, reckless. Make decisions this way, and you are exposing yourself to failure not because you lack the skill or the will, but because you lack the right information.

In the professional sphere, this commitment to truth and integrity is not just a professional responsibility. You are not just deciding for yourself; you are deciding for your team, your organization, and your stakeholders. Whether you are launching a product, negotiating a deal, or leading a project, your decisions shape your future and the future of others. A misstep here, a miscalculation there, and everyone who trusts you stumbles, including your own self. The stakes are high, and the responsibilities are immense. That is why you need credible information to make sound judgments. The same holds true in your personal life, where the decisions you make are no less significant. The food you eat, the exercises you practice, the relationships you choose, the values you uphold – these are the building blocks of your joy. Misinformation here is harmful. It is not just a matter of taste but a matter of well-being and quality of life and the very essence of who you are and what you aspire to be.

The internet, with its infinite resources, is both a boon and a bane. It empowers you with knowledge but exposes you to falsehoods. It opens doors to wisdom but leads you down paths of deception. A study published in Science in 2018 revealed that false information spreads faster and more broadly on social media than true stories. This is the landscape you navigate, the terrain you traverse, filled with promises and pitfalls, with truths and traps. The bottom line is to properly inspect the information you receive and make conscious effort to validate it before actioning based on it.

Social Media

Social media is a tool, and -like any tool- it is how you wield it that determines its impact. Picture yourself navigating a vast, bustling market square. There are shouts from every corner, news from far and wide, opportunities, and connections. Not all the voices are equally trustworthy or relevant to you. On the professional front, you might see businesses leveraging social media to build brand awareness, engage with customers, and even conduct market research. In this case, social media is a hub of innovation where a small business in a remote village can reach global audiences. However, the information maze is not free of pitfalls. According to the MIT report in 2018, false information spreads six times faster on Twitter than the truth. So, imagine a false product review, a twisted piece of news about a competitor, or a misinterpreted tweet. It can affect a company's reputation or lead to misguided business decisions.

Think about how social media shapes your understanding of the world, your connections with friends, your political views, and even your self-image. The social media world has become a window into countless lives and ideas, offering chances to learn, empathize, and grow. But then, there are the echo chambers, those invisible walls that can isolate you from diverse perspectives. What feels like a consensus within your social media circle might be a narrow slice of a broader conversation. An individual's perception of reality can be warped, leading to personal decisions that might not be grounded in comprehensive facts. For example, a study published in the "American Journal of Preventive Medicine" in 2017 showed a strong association between social media use and perceived social isolation among young adults.

So, what is the path forward? Think of it as becoming a skilled market-goer, sharpening your discernment, widening your gaze, and being aware of the invisible walls. Whether you are choosing the right investment based on reliable financial news or understanding a political event from multiple angles, you will need to cultivate an attitude of informed skepticism and openness to various viewpoints. The democratized platforms of social media are neither inherently good nor bad, but mirrors reflecting human nature.

Non-credible published work

In the realm of professional decision-making, relying on false information is akin to steering your ship into perilous waters. Let us say you are a small business owner, and you stumble upon an online article that seems to have the exact insights you need to expand your market reach. However, without proper validation, those insights might turn out to be mere illusions, baseless, and without substance. According to a 2016 study published in the Journal of Economic Perspectives, fake news can distort stock prices and even influence investment behaviors. This can ruin partnerships, erode trust, and send well-laid plans into disarray.

Now, think about health, relationships, education, or lifestyle choices. How often have you sought guidance online for these intimate and significant areas of life? A study conducted by the World Health Organization in 2020 revealed that misinformation related to COVID-19 led to unnecessary panic, stigma, and even health risks. That is how far-reaching and personally damaging these mirages can be. Envisioning these pitfalls is not meant to deter you but rather to sharpen your navigation skills, and ensure that you equip yourself with the right tools and techniques to differentiate between the mirages and the true oases. When seeking professional insights, look for credible sources that adhere to peer-reviewed standards or have been vouched for by experts in the field. Recognize that some sources might wear the mask of credibility but lack the substance. In personal matters, be it seeking medical advice or understanding a cultural nuance, the same principles apply. Go beyond the surface, consult multiple perspectives, cross-verify with authoritative sites, and don't hesitate to seek professional guidance when needed. Be bold to ask questions and investigate further to make sure you are not being misguided.

Bias

Bias is an unseen guide leading you down paths that may *feel* right to you, but are often fraught with peril. In professional settings, this can be likened to a business leader who relies solely on personal experience and instinct without seeking diverse perspectives. I found a study conducted by McKinsey in 2015 proving that companies with diverse executive boards had returns on equity that were 53% higher on average. When decisions are clouded by individual bias that excludes diverse opinions, they tend to overlook new opportunities and creative solutions. Imagine you are part of a critical project, and the person in charge of a critical project has all their decision-making input swayed by personal relationships or prior experiences with team members. This bias may blind them to the talents and potential of others and lead to less-than-optimal performance. A biased perspective limits growth and fosters an environment where innovation is stifled. In relationships, bias shows up where preconceived notions about a friend's behavior clouds judgment and fosters misunderstanding. When it comes to lifestyle choices, bias toward a particular diet or exercise regime, influenced by celebrity endorsements or fleeting trends, lead you to choices that are not aligned with your needs.

The antidote to bias is mindful awareness of your inherent preferences and a conscious effort to broaden your horizons. In the professional world, it means embracing diversity, engaging in constructive dialogues, and being open to challenging established views. In your personal life, it means pausing and questioning why you feel a certain way about someone or something, and genuinely seeking objective information from a wide array of sources, engaging with different viewpoints, and being open to the idea that what feels comfortable is not always what is right for you.

Chapter 6

Forming Possibilities

This is one of the most important questions to answer when it comes to decision-making. You would make sure you are considering every possible alternative, so that you can decide which of them fits your context the most. The more life experience you gain, the more a crossroads in your career or personal life become a familiar experience to you. You are stimulated by a decision, and you already know the familiar paths, those well-trodden routes that feel safe and comfortable, and the less distinct trails, those that beckon you toward something new and different. The latter is the path of creative thinking and forming all possibilities, even if they do not look comfortable. Even if this possibility looks complex, it is one you must understand if you are to make the most out of your life. Remember the limbic system? I am talking about the conflict between the neo-limbic and prefrontal cortex.

Let me bring your attention to another perspective of looking at this. There is a difference between analyzing probabilities, and analyzing possibilities. When you focus on probabilities, it is like using a flashlight in a dark forest; you can only see what's immediately in front of you, which are often the most familiar and safest paths. These are the routes most traveled, where the outcomes are more predictable and often tread upon by those who came before. This gives you a sense of comfort and security, and drives you to stick with well-charted territories. This approach can be comforting, indeed, but can also curtail the horizon of what is achievable.

On the other hand, casting your gaze toward possibilities is akin to climbing a watchtower, giving you a panoramic view of the forest. It is about charting unknown territories, driven by the spirit of exploration and wonder. Here, decisions are molded not by what is typical but by what could be. It's in this realm of possibilities that innovation thrives, dreams take flight, and change-makers emerge. When you commit to exploring possibilities, you permit yourself to dream bigger, to think outside conventions, and to challenge the status quo. It is about seeing a canvas rather than a sketch, and having the audacity to paint your own masterpiece, even if it does not conform to the usual gallery of artworks. Focusing on possibilities is an invitation to embrace the full spectrum of potential outcomes. And so, while the world might operate on tried and tested methods, there is always room for you to reimagine and invent. After all, this book is about exploring who you are to make decisions in the most suitable way to you. And, as unique of a human being as you are, your consideration of possibilities rather than probabilities is what empowers you to explore alternatives that are more suitable to you.

At work, you have probably seen how easy it is to fall into the same patterns. It might be pursuing the same marketing strategy because it worked last year or clinging to a product design simply because it is what has always been done. Unconscious biases and the urge to stay safe silently direct your decisions. If you have ever found yourself leaning toward an idea simply because it came from a senior colleague, that is a bias in action. Social influences, those invisible hands gently push you in a particular direction. If you have ever made a decision at work because that is just "how things are done," that is social influence. I am not calling you to reject these influences; I am highlighting that you need to form possibilities that align with your unique situation and goals.

Personally speaking, think about the last book you read or the last vacation you took. Did you choose them because they fit within your comfort zone? Challenging those comfort boundaries leads you to discover a new favorite author or a hidden travel gem, right? Similarly, if you have ever felt pressured to make a certain life decision because it is what friends or family found to be a more suitable possibility, that is the social influence creeping into your personal life, and acknowledging these influences enables you to make decisions that resonate with *you*, not with those around you.

Biases and social influences, when combined with a comfort zone and tendency to conform, end up with you unconsciously eliminating possibilities that would have actually brought you the most rewarding outcomes. At the end of the day, forming possibilities is all about finding your own way so that you can achieve your life's full potential. In order to do so, you must recognize the biases and social pressures that steer you down familiar paths and learn to navigate them consciously. Professionally, this is what separates the innovators from the followers. Personally, it is what leads to a more fulfilling and authentic existence. It might not be the easiest path, but it is definitely one filled with growth, discovery, and limitless possibilities. Whether you are seeking to grow your business, enhance your career, or nurture your personal relationships, understanding and embracing this journey will help you become the person you aspire to be.

If I have your buy-in now, then you would want to break free from bias, social influences, and comfort to stride toward creativity and growth. The key question here becomes: How can you *objectively* form possibilities?

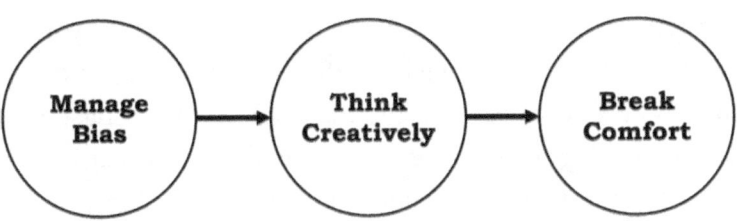

Manage Bias

First things first, you need to identify what is holding you back. Often, your biases and comfort zones are like invisible chains, restraining you from reaching your full potential. What exactly is bias? It is a leaning or inclination that affects your judgment, sometimes without you even realizing it. Bias can influence your thinking in several ways, from the way you make decisions to how you interact with others.

Bias distorts your possibilities in many forms. Cognitive bias affects your reasoning and decision-making. If you have ever made a judgment based on an initial piece of information and ignored everything else, that is anchoring bias at work. This influences your professional choices, like budgeting or negotiating contracts, by making you stick to that first figure you had in mind. Confirmation bias is another trap you might fall into, where you favor information that supports your existing beliefs. If you have ever found yourself ignoring evidence that contradicts your investment decisions or political views, this is confirmation bias in action. You are unconsciously limiting your perspective and this leads to missed opportunities. Gender and racial biases might affect you, too. If you are a hiring manager, are you unintentionally (or intentionally) favoring male or female candidates for certain roles? Are you a teacher with different expectations for students of various ethnicities? These biases influence your professional interactions and personal relationships, and limits your possibilities of making better decisions.

Now, think about your social circle. If you are surrounded by like-minded people, it might feel comforting but it works against your growth. In your professional life, embracing different viewpoints foster creativity and innovation. In your personal life this might mean trying a new social group, volunteering in another community, or traveling somewhere unfamiliar. Ever thought of attending a cultural festival in your town? It could expand your horizons and help reduce cultural biases.

Managing biases is a continual self-awareness exercise. You want to regularly question your thoughts and decisions if you want to achieve a more objective perspective and hence boost your ability of creating possibilities. I invite you to appreciate diversity not just as a concept but as a way of life. From someone who has found true power in staying objective, trust me when I say that recognizing and challenging your biases will push toward a more enlightened, empathetic way of thinking and living. Follow the steps in Exercise 6.1 in the Appendix section whenever you doubt you are being biased while forming possibilities. Also, tools like Implicit Association Tests (IAT) help you discover hidden biases. IAT is available online for free.

Think Creatively

Want to become more creative? Create a safe space for your creative thinking. Imagine trying to brainstorm in a meeting filled with judgment or skepticism. It is stifling, isn't it? To let creativity flourish, you need to place yourself in an environment where encouragement and curiosity reign and new ideas flow freely. Google discovered this in its Project Aristotle, and found that psychological safety greatly enhances team effectiveness. Imagine a design team working on a revolutionary product; they need the freedom to pitch out-of-the-box ideas without fear of ridicule.

You can apply the same logic to your personal life, too. Maybe you are working on a hobby like painting or writing, and you are afraid to try a new style. Encourage creativity within yourself by embracing failure as a learning opportunity. Create art without worrying about it being a masterpiece. It is all about building a culture, whether at your workplace or home, where innovation is not just accepted but celebrated. If you have children, encourage them to think creatively in their school projects and foster a home environment that rewards curiosity and exploration.

Here is a powerful tool for you: Divergent Thinking. In its essence, creativity is not about finding one right answer but exploring multiple unique ideas in all possible directions. In your professional life, you could apply this to product development, marketing strategies, or problem-solving. For example, instead of settling on one marketing strategy, brainstorm various approaches, each tailored to different customer segments. In your personal life, Divergent Thinking might mean exploring different career paths, travel destinations, or even approaches to a relationship challenge. Consider *every* possible route, and analyze what each one could offer, rather than rushing down the first path you see.

Divergent Thinking invites curiosity, flexibility, and playfulness into your problem-solving process, and using it as a creative thinking technique means welcoming the unknown and daring to venture into uncharted territories. Whether you are an entrepreneur launching a start-up, a teacher devising new ways to engage students, or someone just looking to add some spark to everyday life, applying these principles can unlock a more innovative, adventurous you. It is your turn to think creatively and embrace a mindset that celebrates innovation, exploration, and fearless curiosity. Exercises 6.2, 6.3, and 6.4 in the Appendix section will help you form possibilities more creatively.

Break Comfort

Have you had the chance to delve into the pages of Dr. Spencer Johnson's "Who Moved My Cheese?" If not, the story revolves around four mouse-like characters who chance upon a colossal stash of cheese at "Cheese Station C." For Sniff and Scurry, the mouse pair, cheese is their life source, their raison d'être, while for Hem and Haw, it symbolizes security, joy, and triumph. Each day begins with a joyful dance amidst their seemingly endless cheese supply.

Sniff and Scurry's strategies toward their cheese bounty are instinctive and straightforward. Their days start early, sprinting toward Cheese Station C, never assuming that the cheese will always be there for their taking. Alert and grounded, they're ready to adapt at a moment's notice. Hem and Haw, on the other hand, build their lives around the cheese, making their home near it, setting routines, and anchoring their identities and self-worth to the abundant cheese. As all good things must come to an end, so does their cheese stockpile. The vigilant pair, Sniff and Scurry, are quick to sense the dwindling cheese supply, recognizing the inevitable truth that the cheese will soon be no more. They aren't taken aback or disheartened when the day of cheese scarcity arrives. They simply dust themselves off and set out in search of new cheese, displaying admirable resilience in the face of change. Hem and Haw, who have grown complacent, are staggered by the cheese's absence. They feel a profound sense of betrayal. Hem becomes resentful and resists the idea of seeking new cheese, stubbornly clinging to his old reality.

Haw, though initially hesitant, begins to entertain the possibility of change. He faces a dilemma: to stick with the familiar or venture out searching for new cheese. It is a moment of choice, one that asks him to step out of his comfort zone, take a risk, and open himself to new lessons. One day, he gathers the courage to step into the unknown, leaving behind Hem, who continues to deny reality. As Haw navigates the daunting maze alone, he grapples with his deepest fears. His journey is marked by numerous falls and dead ends, but each setback serves as a lesson. Along the maze walls, he leaves behind messages such as "What would you do if you weren't afraid?" reflecting his acceptance of change. After a multitude of trials and errors, Haw finally discovers "Cheese Station N," brimming with fresh cheese, even more abundant than before. He's overjoyed and relieved, yet also mindful that he must remain alert for future changes. He periodically explores the maze, ready for the next shift. He nurtures hope that Hem might eventually embrace change and find the new cheese. Meanwhile, Hem continues to remain stuck in his past, resistant to move on.

Now, let us pivot from this parable to the real world and examine the life of the renowned billionaire Richard Branson, founder of the Virgin Group, which today spans over 400 companies in diverse sectors. Branson was born in England in 1950 and battled severe learning difficulties in his early life. He had dyslexia, which posed substantial challenges in his academics. But even these obstacles could not dampen his entrepreneurial spirit. At the tender age of 16, Branson dropped out of school to start a youth culture magazine called "Student." It was an unconventional path and a choice that required him to step out of his comfort zone and face social pressure. The magazine enjoyed some success, but it did not generate sufficient revenue to sustain the business. Branson was never the one to shy away from taking risks, and he decided to sell mail-order records through the magazine. This venture turned out to be a tremendous success and led to the establishment of Virgin Records in the 1970s. But Branson was far from complacent. He resolved to step into the cutthroat airline industry.

With zero experience in aviation, he leased a single Boeing 747 and launched Virgin Atlantic. It was a bold step outside his comfort zone and one fraught with considerable risks. Branson remained resolute despite skepticism from many, including his own team. He introduced his unique Virgin flair to the airline, offering superior customer service and novel in-flight experiences. Soon, Virgin Atlantic was rubbing shoulders with established companies like British Airways. Today, Virgin Atlantic is one of the world's leading airlines, a testament to Branson's daring move outside his comfort zone. But Branson did not stop there. He continuously pushed the boundaries, venturing into telecommunications with Virgin Mobile, fitness with Virgin Active, and even space tourism with Virgin Galactic.

Listen, I am not sure what keeps you in your comfort zone, and I am not saying that staying in it is necessarily bad. I am sure you have good reasons for not willing to explore further possibilities, if that is the case. This decision is completely up to you. My role, however, is to make sure you realize what you are missing out on. To make sure I have done this, I have one last example to share with you, and it is a quick story about two lions. The first is caged within the confines of a zoo, his every need attended to — from food to medical care and shelter. It lives under the constant gaze of spectators in return for his survival being ensured. It is safe. The other, a king in the wild, lives a life of uncertainty yet enjoys boundless freedom to do as he pleases. It is free.

Your comfort zone is that sweet spot where you function in an anxiety-neutral environment, cruising through familiar tasks with ease and security. Your activities follow a predictable pattern, and

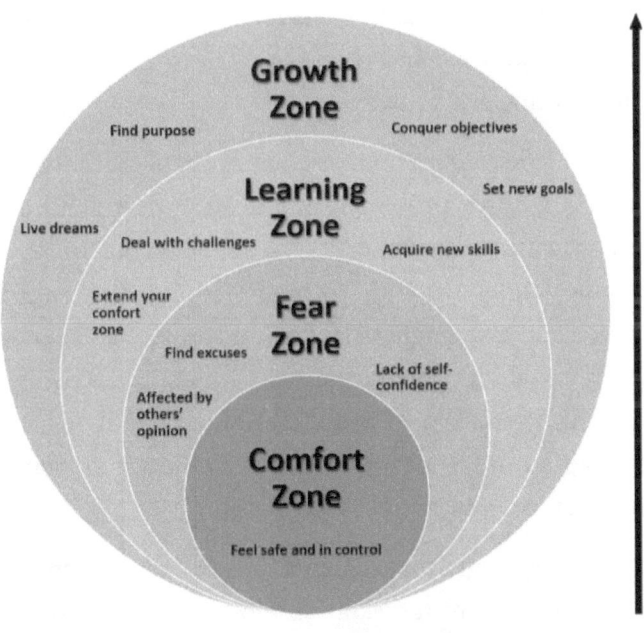

you remain cocooned from stress and risk. This is a behavioral haven where you can conduct your routine seamlessly, undisturbed by the threat of high anxiety. But don't be fooled, my friend. This comfort zone, despite its emotional security, can morph into a self-imposed prison. A theory that has been around since 1908, proposed by psychologists Robert M.

Yerkes and John D. Dodson, puts forth the concept of 'optimal anxiety.' They posit that a comfortable state fosters a steady, but not necessarily peak, level of performance. For that, a hint of anxiety is necessary, pushing you just beyond the edges of your comfort zone into an 'optimal anxiety' zone. It is a delicate balance, though; too much anxiety can backfire, resulting in plummeting performance due to overwhelming stress.

The sphere of 'optimal anxiety' borders on what we term the 'fear zone,' a realm where anxiety reigns, potentially causing feelings of overwhelm and inhibiting optimal performance. It is a zone filled with trepidation and worry, often manifested through procrastination, excuses, and an immobilizing sensation of being stuck. More often than not, this fear zone forms a daunting barrier, preventing you from stepping outside your comfort zone and propelling you toward spaces of genuine growth – the learning and growth zones.

In the 'learning zone,' the game changes. This is where you rise to challenges, solve problems, and acquire new skills and abilities. Rather than viewing mistakes as failures, they're seen as essential feedback, stepping stones on your path to learning. Entering this zone requires courage and a willingness to face uncertainty and potential mistakes. It is the arena where genuine growth begins. A study by Professor Alison Wood Brooks from Harvard Business School suggests that those who perceive stress as an opportunity for learning demonstrate improved performance in high-stakes situations.

But the magic truly happens in the 'growth zone.' This is the space where you cement the skills and lessons harvested in the learning zone. This is the playground of perpetual development, where you set and achieve goals, live in alignment with your values, and constantly embrace new challenges. Here, you are operating at your full potential. A study from the University at Buffalo demonstrated that mild stress and anxiety levels can stimulate brain activity and boost performance.

Your comfort zone might offer a pleasant rest stop, but it is not where your life thrives. Your human nature might gravitate toward comfort but growth and development bloom when you dare to step outside these boundaries. The journey through the fear zone, into the learning zone, and finally, the growth zone is integral to personal and professional evolution. The goal is not to live in a state of perpetual stress but rather to seek out meaningful and rewarding challenges. As author Neale Donald Walsch poignantly said, "life begins at the end of your comfort zone." I cannot express how getting used to being free and norming to welcome change and challenges with open arms is the most empowering and valuable character-building exercise you can take yourself through.

Realizing comfort

You might be reading the previous paragraphs and believing you are already way out of your comfort zone. It is quite intriguing how we often miss the obvious. There are numerous reasons why the realization of your own comfort might elude you, but topping that list is a uniquely human characteristic - your innate ability to adapt and habituate over time. You see, this adaptation is fundamentally a survival mechanism and a clever trick evolution has handed down to you. It equips you to acclimate, withstand, and navigate varying environments, whether they are draped in comfort or stripped of it. But here is the twist: This same adaptive tendency also means you can unknowingly become ensnared within a relatively narrow and familiar bouquet of experiences. You may recognize this as the 'comfort zone.' It is such a subtle transition that you may not even notice you have been ensnared.

Your comfort zone's contours are often defined by your day-to-day routines and patterns. These rituals, repeated over time, become so ingrained and woven into the fabric of your life, that they turn invisible. Carried out almost mechanically, these routines demand little conscious thought. Only when the rhythm of your life is disrupted when you are jolted out of your routines or compelled to modify them, do you truly discern how snugly you were nestled in your comfort zone. It is intriguing, isn't it, how you may chart your life's course or make decisions just because they are perceived as the norm? Think this way, and you allow these choices to shepherd you, quite subtly, into the warmth of your comfort zones. Yet, precisely because these paths are so ubiquitously followed, you might fail to recognize them as comfort zones. The cloak of normalcy can often mask the reality of comfortable confinement.

The key takeaway of this long argument about comfort is to help you understand the value of conscious self-awareness, and to recognize the boundaries of your comfort zones and the routine patterns that constitute them. There is nothing inherently wrong with comfort zones. They serve as psychological safety nets and provide security and predictability. However, as we discussed earlier, the essence of personal growth lies in the ability to step outside these comfort zones. Therefore, it is not about vilifying comfort zones but about understanding their limits and the potential benefits of stepping beyond them. So, how about venturing out a bit? If you want to explore further how attached you are to your comfort zone, give Exercise 6.5 in the Appendix section a go.

You might be thinking now, "This guy is completely ignoring mental health and traumas and makes breaking out of comfort zones and facing fears sound easy. What does he know?!" Yes, you are right. Traumas do differ from limiting beliefs, but they share one important thing in common: they both have the power to limit your potential and overshadow your authentic self. Trauma, in case you are not quite familiar with the word, is the complex reaction to a distressing or life-threatening event that involves both your mind and body. It can come about as a result of a variety of experiences - think physical or emotional abuse, violence, accidents, natural disasters, or exposure to combat. These traumatic incidents can overwhelm one's ability to cope, shaking one's sense of safety, control, and overall well-being. I am human, and just like everyone else, have had my share of traumas.

When you go through a traumatic event, both your brain and body undergo physiological changes as part of the stress response. This involves the activation of your sympathetic nervous system, which leads to the release of stress hormones like adrenaline and cortisol. These hormones get your body ready for a "fight-or-flight" reaction, accelerating your heart rate, blood pressure, and alertness. In the heat of a traumatic event, your brain's amygdala—the part of your brain that plays a crucial role in processing emotions—can become unusually active. This heightened activity might hinder your brain's ability to properly process and integrate the traumatic experience. As a result, your memories of the traumatic event could end up fragmented, disorganized, or encoded differently in your brain compared to non-traumatic memories. The hippocampus, another part of your brain involved in memory formation, can also bear the brunt of trauma. Chronic stress and elevated cortisol levels can result in the hippocampus shrinking, leading to difficulties in consolidating and retrieving memories related to traumatic events. What is more, trauma can affect the prefrontal cortex of your brain, the part responsible for executive functions like decision-making, emotional regulation, and impulse control. While the prefrontal cortex helps to moderate the stress response, trauma can impair its functioning, making it harder for you to regulate emotions and deal with stress. Several factors, such as your genetic makeup, previous experiences, the social support you have, and your resilience, influence how you react to and cope with traumatic events. Moreover, the impact of trauma might extend beyond your psyche, affecting your physical health, relationships, and overall well-being.

If you find yourself relating to what I have just explained about traumas, I strongly urge you to consult a therapist or a clinical psychologist. Reading books about traumas and hoping to get better is like reading books about headaches and expecting the pain to go away. Reading might help you understand your traumas, but it is unlikely to be enough to heal them. What matters is that you take responsibility for your mental health and solve whatever issues you might have, and not let yourself be a Victim and to stay safe in your comfort zone.

Part 3 – The Decision Moment

*"The audacity to decide is the alchemy that transforms the fog of uncertainty
into the gold of clarity."*

Chapter 7

The 'Right' Decision

You are in mid-18th century France, precisely in 1738. It is a turbulent time with enlightenment ideas bubbling up, challenging the old norms and traditions, and amongst the thinkers of the time, there is one mathematician who stands out: Gabriel Cramer. Although Cramer is known for his contributions to algebra and mathematics and is considered to be a historical figure, there is a personal quirk that makes him incredibly relatable. Cramer was a worrier, plagued by the fear of loss and failure. It might seem strange for someone of his brilliance, but worry is a very human trait.

One day, a wealthy merchant in Geneva proposes a game of chance to Cramer and his equally brilliant friend, Nicholas Bernoulli. It was a deceptively simple game, one that will pit Cramer's mathematical mind against his anxiety. The game was about a flipped coin. If the flip is heads, Cramer would win a certain amount, but if it is tails, he would lose. The merchant sets the odds, the possible winnings, and the potential losses. Now, you might be thinking, "Why would a mathematician, a thinker, and a man of logic entertain such a gamble?". That is where the expected utility theory came into play. Cramer sat down and began to apply this theory to his decision. He weighed the potential gains against the possible losses. But he was not looking at them in isolation, rather considering his own feelings, his own fears, and his aversion to risk. He was using the expected utility theory as a tool to make this decision not just logically but also emotionally. He calculated and calculated, trying to explore his own soul and his own values. He was trying to find that balance between the cold numbers and the warm, irrational, human part of himself. In the end, he turned down the gamble, and he did so with clarity and a peace that he would not have had without this theory. His fear of loss and his risk aversion played into his decision-making.

Nicholas Bernoulli, who was watching all of this, wrote to his cousin, Daniel Bernoulli, about Cramer's decision. Bernoulli was already working on his groundbreaking paper on risk and utility, and found inspiration in Cramer's struggle. Cramer's decision became a historical moment and a spark that helped shape one of the fundamental theories in economics and decision-making.

This is how the expected utility theory serves as both a mathematical tool and a philosophical guide at the same time, making it a way to understand

Expected Utility

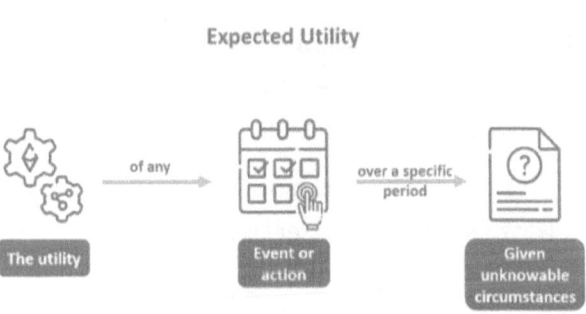

yourself better and helping you bridge between your logic and your emotions. This is like walking a tightrope toward a goal, with different outcomes on each side, each holding its own allure and risk. This approach, first introduced by Daniel Bernoulli in 1738, is still widely used in economics and psychology today. The approach bridges between the numbers, cold fact, complex reality, and the human heart's desires and fears. The approach is simple: you need to acknowledge that you are not just logically considering potential gains or losses but also how you feel about them. If you were investing money, for example, it wouldn't just be about how much you might gain or lose but how comfortable you are with the level of risk involved.

Then comes the probabilities, your best guess at how likely each result is. For a parable, imagine you are planning a garden, and you have a handful of seeds. Each type of plant represents a different outcome, and the chance of them growing successfully varies. You might love roses, but if they only have a 10% chance of thriving in your garden, you would have to consider that in your decision. So, you take all these factors, your love for roses, and their chance of growing, and you multiply them together. You do this for each choice you have and sum up these products to give you an overall value for each option. It is like having a shopping list of all the different plants, their prices, and their likelihood of flourishing, and then calculating the total value you'd get from each. The choice with the highest expected utility is the one you go for. Now, let us say you are using this theory in a more professional context, like deciding on a career path. The calculation does not end with considering the salary or the job title but also what you value in your work and life, like your passion, your family, your well-being, and how all of these align with the potential paths.

The question to ask now, I believe, is: How can you be in control of this whole process, to make sure your perspective is objectively balanced between your logical analysis of a potential decision and its possibilities, and how you feel about the decision in your guts? To answer this question for both you and I, I have designed the IVIC Decision-Making Framework©.

The IVIC Decision-Making Framework©

How can you be confident in your skin, in control of your perspectives, and eventually make your decisions and live your life the way you want? My strategy is to proactively become aware of who you are and what you want even before you are put into the position of making a decision. This strategy empowers you to have the clarity and confidence needed to make the right decision, regardless of the pressure or uncertainty that comes along with it, and despite any external influence. This is the strategy upon which I have designed the IVIC Decision-Making Framework©.

IVIC Decision-Making Framework©

IVIC Decision-Making Framework© is a reliable tool crafted after years of psychological research and experience, and designed to infuse your decision-making journey with clarity, authenticity, and confidence. IVIC is the abbreviation of the four pillars upon which the framework was built:

1. Identity: Which choice expresses who I am?
2. Vision: Which choice do I want?
3. Impact: Which choice empowers me to make the biggest impact?
4. Cost: Which choice can I afford?

The first pillar of this framework, Identity, is the foundation on which you construct your decisions. Rooted in the psychological theory of self-concept, this pillar involves a deep dive into understanding who you truly are - your perspectives, motives, values, passion, abilities, and mission in life. A strong understanding of your identity will lead you to greater decisiveness and consistency in your decision-making behavior. This clarity about your identity helps you to eliminate options that do not resonate with your authentic self, and you become more able to narrow down the field and simplify your possibilities more easily.

The second pillar, Vision, is your beacon in the fog of decision-making. Grounded in purpose and mission, your vision reflects the path you have charted out to get there. The field of positive psychology emphasizes the importance of having a clear direction in promoting overall well-being and satisfaction. In decision-making, your vision acts as a reference point and helps you evaluate how each possibility could aid or hinder your journey toward your goal.

The Impact pillar gauge the potential effect of each possibility. Here, cognitive psychology comes into play, underscoring the importance of evaluating the potential outcomes of your choices. Since you have already checked your identity and your vision as priorities, it is time to think of the wider ecosystem. Back to the Butterfly Effect, as I have explained in the introduction, your decisions do impact nature and other people's lives, and any decision you make will have consequences that will end up disrupting the world in a way or another. So, why not make this disruption intentionally positive for the rest of us?

Finally, the Cost pillar is about bringing your attention to weigh the trade-offs associated with each possibility. This step is rooted in economic and decision theory and urges you to consider what you stand to lose or gain with each choice. Let us examine each pillar in depth. Generally, I have attached a worksheet in the Appendix section (Exercise 7.1) to help you work on the IVIC model, but I strongly suggest you have a full understanding of this part of the book first before you can make the best out of the exercise.

Chapter 8

The Authentic Possibility

In 2017, I was standing at a life-altering crossroads in Egypt. The shimmering mirage of opportunity had unveiled itself to me in the form of a lucrative job offer in Dubai, a land known for its sandy dunes and towering skyscrapers, a beacon of modernity and progress. The proposal

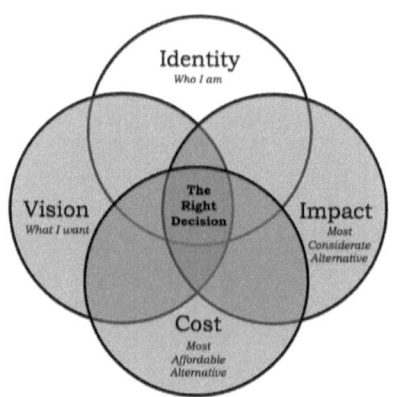

IVIC Decision-Making Framework©

was enticing, to say the least. It was a call to a thriving, dynamic city that promised both an uptick in financial stability and the prospect of accelerated career progression. It felt like a vast, well-lit path spreading out before me, beckoning me toward a brighter future and a destiny carved in gold. At the same time, my father's health was declining back home. It felt like I have to choose whether to capture the opportunity for myself, or stay with my family and care for my father until he is well.

So, there I was, stuck in the middle of an emotional tug of war, torn between a promising career in a city and my duty to my sick father. Both options had their own weight and gravity. As days turned into weeks, the decision loomed larger, casting a lengthening shadow over my daily life. I discovered the complex emotional tapestry that accompanies such life-changing decisions. I felt the thrill of a new opportunity, the anxiety of leaving a familiar setting, the responsibility toward my family, and the uncertainty of the future.

But amid all the turmoil and confusion, there was also a strange sense of clarity. In grappling with my predicament, I was forced to confront my values, my fears, and my dreams while learning to navigate the labyrinth of emotions that came with it. It was a journey of self-discovery that went beyond the simple act of making a choice, taking me on a deep dive into the realms of decision-making and emotion management. And that is just it, isn't it? Decisions, especially the life-changing ones, are usually never straightforward. They are tangled webs of emotions, values, aspirations, and responsibilities. But through the struggle, they offer a unique opportunity to learn, to grow, and to truly understand what matters. So, while I stood there on the precipice of a life-changing decision, I realized that no matter what choice I would make, I had already gained something invaluable – insight into my own self.

You must familiarize yourself with who you are if you want to have the clarity and confidence to make complex decisions. Embrace your values and identity, then match possibilities with them. Only then can you stand firm in your decisions and move forward without looking back, only then can you truly live. In a study published in the Journal of Adult Development, researchers found that individuals with high self-awareness tend to make more decisive and consistent choices. Similarly, a study in the Harvard Business Review discovered that CEOs with strong self-awareness had companies with higher ROIs and workforce satisfaction rates. This is clear evidence of how self-awareness, your dependable GPS, ensures you are making decisions that lead you on the right path for you and others. I invite you to explore what might be at the core of this hesitation to uncover the fundamental fears that shape who you are and how you approach life's challenges.

If we agree that your decisions are your life's building blocks, then taking control of how you make your decisions is common sense. It is not the first step, though. A prerequisite to taking control of your life, and so the way you make decisions, is to know how you want your life to look like in the first place. To gain clarity about the direction and design of your life is profoundly intertwined with understanding yourself deeply. The essence of determining how your life should look is not just about chasing external milestones, accolades, or societal norms. Instead, it is about aligning your life with the core of who they truly are. Discovering who you are is like setting a foundation for a building. The sturdier and more profound this foundation, the more resilient and authentic the structure that you build upon it. If you are unsure about your perspectives, motives, values, passions, abilities, and mission in life, any decisions you make or paths you pursue might end up feeling hollow and unfulfilling, no matter how much external success they bring.

Think of it like trying to choose a destination without understanding what kind of terrain you thrive in. You might end up on a beach when you are truly a mountain person, or in a bustling city when your heart seeks the tranquility of the countryside. Understanding yourself involves introspection and reflection. This is about asking challenging questions and seeking honest answers: What do you believe in? What drives you? What values are non-negotiable for you? What ignites your passion? What are you capable of? What environments make you feel the most alive and in alignment? Defining these facets of your identity helps you carve out a life path that feels genuine. When you have a clear sense of who you are, decisions about how your life should look become more intuitive. For instance, if you recognize that you are someone who values close-knit relationships over career advancement, you will choose jobs and places that allow you to stay close to family and friends. If you know deep down that creativity is a driving force for you, then even if you are in a conventional job, you will find ways to infuse creativity into your tasks or pursue creative passions on the side. In essence, knowing yourself is the compass guiding you through life's vast possibilities. It provides the criteria against which you can evaluate opportunities and challenges, ensuring that the life you build is a genuine reflection of your true self. With this self-awareness, you not only find direction but also cultivate a life imbued with meaning, purpose, and personal satisfaction. For this, I have designed The Authenticity Pyramid©.

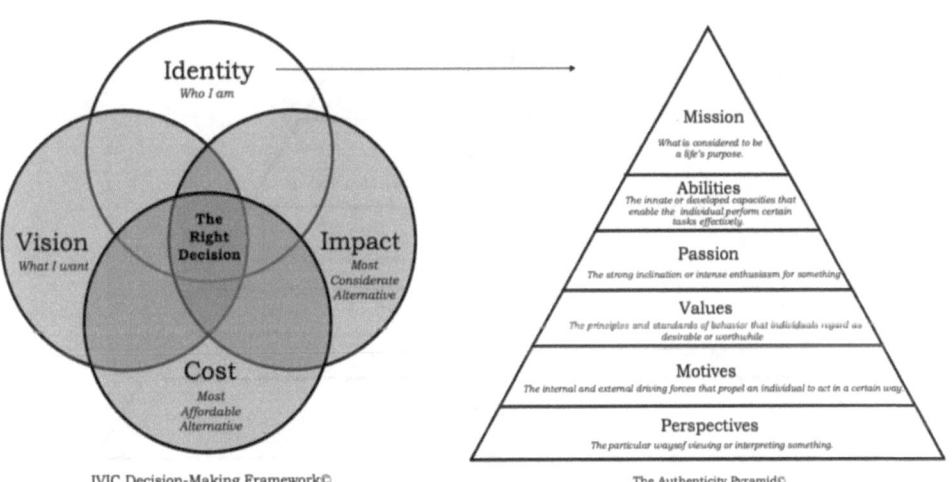

IVIC Decision-Making Framework©   The Authenticity Pyramid©

The Authenticity Pyramid©

Visualize the journey of self-awareness as a pyramid—an ascending, hierarchical structure leading to the pinnacle of self-realization. I fondly refer to this as The Authenticity Pyramid©, an original framework I designed for my clients to boost self-awareness and gain the confidence and clarity they aspire to have.

The Authenticity Pyramid©

Your self-awareness starts with you understanding your own perspectives. Every decision you make, and every interaction you have is colored by this unique perspective. Rise to the next level, and you start exploring your motives. These are the drivers and invisible hands pushing and pulling you toward or away from decisions. Often, these motives operate subtly, influencing you without your explicit knowledge. To navigate your path, you must expose these hidden forces. Are they born out of fear or love? Power or compassion? When you realize your hidden motives, you can define what your values are. These are your non-negotiables. Your values govern your behavior, shaping your actions and reactions. Aligning your decisions with your values ensures that your decisions resonate with who you are and provides you with a sense of inner peace.

When you have explored the deepest levels of who you are, you start moving towards a more dynamic layer of your identity. These are sides of your personality that change multiple times throughout your life. Your passions are those activities or pursuits that light the fire in your heart and make you lose track of time. Decisions aligned with your passions are often imbued with a sense of purpose, a feeling of rightness that is hard to replicate. Your abilities are the realm of your skills, your talents, and your strengths. These are the tools in your arsenal and the resources you have at your disposal. Knowing your abilities intimately is a key to unlocking your potential, and plays the role of a catalyst for confidence and competence. When you are aware of your abilities and decide to believe in them, your confidence is boosted in ambiguous circumstances. Finally, when you have become fairly aware of all of these layers of who you are, you are able to define your life's mission—your purpose in life. Your mission is not necessarily a grand plan or a monumental task but a compass guiding your life toward purposeful action. When your decisions align with your life mission, they transform from being tactical or socially-influenced action into meaningful steps on your journey of self-fulfillment. If you have not had this yet, let me tell you that without having a mission, you are missing out on a massive chance to make confident and meaningful decisions.

Every layer of The Authenticity Pyramid© guides you further on your path toward self-awareness, providing you with the tools to make authentic, value-aligned, and purposeful decisions. This chapter will help you define the first 3 layers of the pyramid, to help decide which of the possibilities is more aligned with your identity as a person. The following chapter will take you through the upper 3 layers of the pyramid, and guide you to narrow down your probabilities even further by deciding which of them empowers you to build the life you want. And, of course, I will equip you with self-coaching tools and exercises to further help you reach answers. I have to say, though, that you might still need personalized help in figuring out a few clouded areas or decluttering a distorted perspective. The purpose of this book is to bring your attention to related matters you might not be paying enough attention to. If you believe you still need more clarity, I am always available to have a coaching conversation and help you find the clarity you seek.

Your Perspectives

During the early morning hours of July 23rd, 1952, a group of Egyptian army officers led by the Free Officers Movement orchestrated a coup, ousting King Farouk I of Egypt and Sudan. This unexpected turn of events marked the demise of the monarchy and set the stage for the establishment of the Republic of Egypt. At the forefront of this transformative period in Middle Eastern history stood Gamal Abdel Nasser, the historically charismatic leader and the driving force behind the Free Officers Movement. Nasser governed Egypt with unwavering control and a vision for a promising future. However, beneath the scenes, a mysterious influence was at play, manipulating the minds of the populace and exerting control over the dissemination of information.

During Nasser's regime, the Egyptian press teemed with diverse opinions and ideas, reflecting the nation's vibrant intellectual landscape. With the monarchy's fall, people hoped to exercise freedom of speech, believing that democracy was within reach. Yet, as time passed, rumors began to circulate among journalists and editors regarding a clandestine group known as the Watchmen. Whispers suggested that these enigmatic figures possessed the power to manipulate the very words printed and spoken throughout the land. Selected from Nasser's most devoted followers, the watchful gaze of these Watchmen extended across the entire media landscape.

The Watchmen tightened their hold on Egypt's media, and the once-lively press gradually lost its vibrancy. Journalists who dared to challenge the official narrative faced suppression, their voices silenced, careers ruined, and some even imprisoned within Nasser's dark dungeons. The Watchmen, with their ability to edit, censor, or halt any publication or broadcast, instilled fear and uncertainty among journalists. Published works were subject to alterations or outright rejection. Remaining journalists succumbed to a chilling form of self-censorship. They meticulously revised their words in their minds, aware that their work would be scrutinized and modified. Yes, the Watchmen had successfully seized control over the minds of the journalists. When Nasser passed away, the physical Watchmen ceased to exist. However, the mental Watchmen in the minds of journalists endured. Journalists had already become mentally programmed to think and advocate for censored opinions, without needing a Watchman to censor their work. Egyptians had been conditioned to think, act, and speak in a prescribed manner, while society emotionally assassinated anyone who dared to deviate from the established norms.

What similarities do you see between the Watchmen in the above story and the society you interact with every day? I am asking because, if we had to draw a parallel to the limbic system operations we have covered earlier, think of your perspectives as the maestro conducting an intricate neural orchestra. Your perspectives hold the baton, influencing how the symphony of decision-making plays out in your mind. If a fact or situation is perceived as a threat, your Reptilian Complex takes center stage, stirring up a tumultuous symphony of defensive and protective actions. On the other hand, if you perceive the fact or situation as an opportunity, your in-house visionary Prefrontal Cortex steps forward to guide the orchestra, encouraging the composition of positive and constructive decisions. You will find yourself in a dilemma if you keep thinking of society as a Watchman who is going to condemn you if you do not believe in what it believes. But, when you choose to believe that you are free and able to make decisions the way you want, you become a leadership figure and inspire society with your authenticity and boldness.

You take charge of your decision-making process when you fully understand this elaborate cognitive ballet. When you are faced with a decision, do not rush making it to achieve relief. Instead, pause and introspect. Examine your belief system and question your perspectives. If you are intimidated by society's perspective of this situation, know that you are capable of rebuilding your perspectives upon

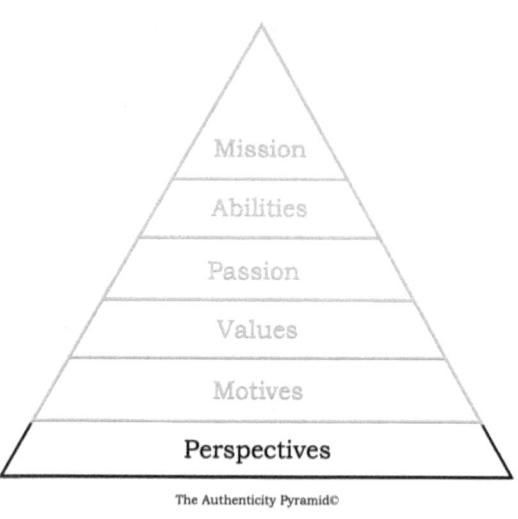

The Authenticity Pyramid©

your confidence in what you believe. Ask yourself if your perspectives are fear-based or opportunity-oriented. Check if they are colored by past experiences or fueled by future aspirations. This simple act of introspection can help ensure that your decisions align with your true, authentic self, and are not just reflexive responses to a distorted perception of facts. Your belief system holds the power to shape your decisions, so make sure it is tuned to your authentic self. Tune in, introspect, and let your decisions be a reflection of who you truly are, not just a mirror of your perceptions. You know what, dear friend? This Watchman you are afraid of, does not really exist. Most of what prevents you from embracing your authentic self-boils down to one word: People. Your caregivers, influenced by their societal conditioning, projected their experiences onto you. Your school teachers, with their personal biases, transferred their beliefs to you. The act of influencing thoughts is, at its core, an exercise of control. The more you allow outside influences to shape your thinking, the more control you surrender. The result? A blurring of personal boundaries and a diminished sense of self-worth. The goal is not to vilify society or challenge the concept of societal norms, but to encourage you to practice the freedom of being your true self irrespective of societal expectations.

Think about those moments when you worried about how others perceived you or when you struggled to strike a balance between being politically correct and standing your ground. Reflect on the difference in your comfort level when anonymously commenting on a social media post versus giving face-to-face feedback at work. These examples reveal how societal influences can impact your decision-making process and how crucial it is to navigate these influences to be true to yourself. If you are still with me, then you might be interested in exploring what all of this means to you. Exercise 8.1 in the Appendix section is a series of reflection questions that aim to help you think and reflect on your own belief system.

My dear friend, I encourage you to appreciate the potential risks of a rigid mindset. When you fiercely cling to society-created narratives and reject the reality around you, you hinder your own self-development, let slip important opportunities, and could potentially inflict harm on yourself and those around you. It is both sensible and healthy to scrutinize your beliefs, assess their alignment with the real world, and be open to modifying them when new information comes to light. I am not suggesting that you lead a life purely in response to your own interpretation of external events. Rather, what I am emphasizing is the importance of finding balance. You should hold onto the beliefs that align with your true self while simultaneously staying receptive to the ever-changing landscape of the world. This balance is pivotal if you earnestly want to witness personal and professional growth. Cultivate a mindset of intellectual curiosity, humility, and a readiness to question your own presuppositions. This mindset is key to realistically navigating life and making choices that are anchored in truth. This way, you make sure that your decisions are authentic and do reflect your own will, not someone else's.

Your Motives

Malala Yousafzai, the Pakistani activist for female education, is the youngest-ever Nobel Prize laureate. In 2009, Taliban had taken control of Malala's home region in Pakistan, and banned girls from attending school. Malala is a person motivated by purpose, and this was a direct affront to her deep-seated view: the right to education and gender equality. Motivated, Malala decided to voice her resistance, and started blogging anonymously for the BBC about life under the Taliban regime and her desire to go to school. This decision was fraught with danger since the Taliban was known for their violent reprisals against dissenters. Yet, her compelling motives led her to make a decision that placed her in harm's way.

Her motives did not waver even after she was targeted and shot by the Taliban in 2012. Once she recovered, Malala only intensified her advocacy for girls' education. She co-authored a book, delivered a speech to the United Nations, and started a fund to support girls' education. This is what I call a motivated person! Malala's decisions, from blogging for the BBC to starting an international fund, were all driven by her intrinsic motives. She was not looking for fame or money, or else she would have taken a different path to achieve those. Her motives were truly authentic.

A person sets the alarm for a brisk 5 AM, even though their day does not formally start until 9 AM. They have no urgent meetings and no unfinished tasks, just an arduous workout session waiting. And there they are, leaving the warmth of their bed, embracing the chill of the early morning, and pushing their body to the limit. Why? Their motive might be to maintain their health, to look a certain way, or to feel that kick start of energy that sets the rhythm for the rest of their day. In the world of psychology, motives are often referred to as the 'why' behind your actions - the internal or external drives that influence your decisions and behaviors. Motives form the underlying framework that guides your choices, propels your actions, and shapes your life's course.

Your motives are closely intertwined with your belief system. Actually, your motives are the product of what you believe in. Authentic belief systems serve as a solid foundation for genuine motives. For instance, if you genuinely believe in lifelong learning, your

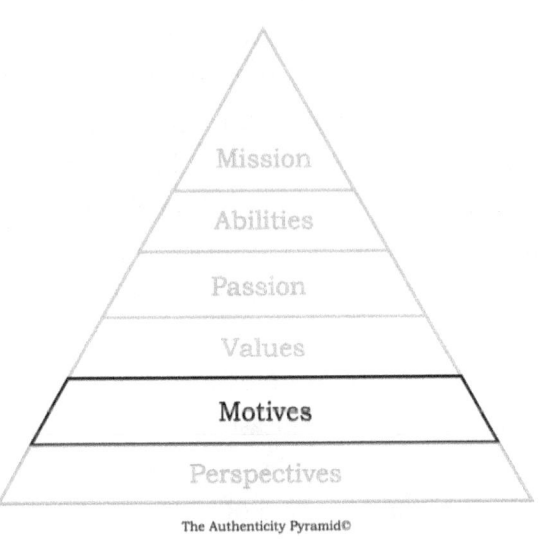

The Authenticity Pyramid©

motive to sign up for that advanced course comes naturally, even amidst a busy schedule. Imagine you are a team leader overseeing a crucial project. You regularly put in extra hours to ensure its success, often compromising on personal time. Here, your motive could be your commitment to excellence, the thrill of achieving challenging targets, or perhaps the promise of a promotion. Your authentic belief in the value of hard work and achievement fuels these motives. So, to truly understand your actions and predict your future decisions, you need to have a solid understanding of what motivates you. Being aware of why you do what you do is a vital step in making authentic decisions. You are more likely to make decisions aligned with your true self this way.

Broadly speaking, there are two types of motives: intrinsic and extrinsic. Each plays a unique role in shaping your actions and decisions. Intrinsic motives are the ones that reside deep within you, like a hidden treasure waiting to be unearthed. They are your soul's callings that often provide a powerful driving force. Is it curiosity that propels you? Do you find yourself seeking out novel experiences and knowledge, embracing them as stepping stones to self-growth? Or perhaps it is the thrill of a challenge that stirs a sense of adventure within you, encouraging you to tackle complex tasks and problems. It might be the pursuit of mastery that drives you, pushing you to strive for competence in specific areas. Maybe it is the need for self-expression that becomes your canvas for artistic or creative release, or the yearning for personal growth and development that forms the bedrock of your desire for continuous evolution. Altruism might allow your heart to experience the joy of contributing to society, while the desire for autonomy might fuel your need for independence and self-direction. A deep enthusiasm or interest could spark your passion, transforming work into pleasure. The need for affiliation may reflect your pursuit of close relationships or community involvement, and the desire to achieve a purpose that holds deep personal significance for you may offer a sense of fulfillment. Intrinsic motives are tied closely to your perspectives. When your actions align with your authentic beliefs, the journey becomes more enjoyable and fruitful.

Extrinsic motives are external factors that compel you to act. This could be the desire for a pay raise, recognition, or the approval of others. While they can be powerful drivers, the 1999 research published by the American Journal of Psychology suggests that a reliance on extrinsic motives can sometimes undermine your intrinsic motivation. You are often influenced by external factors, and play a crucial role in your decision-making. Financial rewards may drive you in your pursuit of higher salaries, bonuses, or other monetary incentives. Is it the quest for recognition that inspires you to work harder, craving acknowledgment or praise from others? Perhaps you wish for a higher social standing or reputation, which manifests as a desire for social status, or you feel the need to influence or control others, reflecting a craving for power. Maybe career advancement is an appealing motive for you, beckoning you toward promotion or professional growth. The need for security, whether financial, professional, or personal, often drives decisions. It might be peer approval that guides your actions, or the hope to gain acceptance from a specific group. Compliance with societal norms, traditions, or regulations is often a motive that nudges you to fit into societal expectations. The avoidance of punishment can be a powerful deterrent, steering your decisions away from potential negative consequences. Lastly, the spirit of competition might be a familiar motive for you, pushing you to strive to outperform others in various fields.

And so, when you construct your life around genuine beliefs, your intrinsic motives gain more strength. Your drive to do things comes from a place of authenticity rather than compulsion or the need for external validation, and now is about time that you reflect on your own motives. What drives your decisions and actions? Are they mostly intrinsic, fueled by your passions? Or extrinsic, influenced by external rewards? As you step forward on this path of understanding your motives, you are taking a pivotal step toward making conscious decisions on which you have fully control. Exercise 8.2 in the Appendix section will help you understand yourself better in this area.

Your Values

A client I once worked with, whom I will call John for the sake of this discussion, was an educated, charming, and attractive personality. Yet, he strongly believed that his lack of success in the dating world and his inability to find love was solely due to his height. This belief held such power over him that even the slightest cues were interpreted as rejection. Consequently, he barely made any effort to meet women, leading to a self-fulfilling prophecy where his dating life indeed suffered. The root of the issue was that John had unwittingly chosen a value - height - that disempowered him and sabotaged his potential for connection and happiness. He became caught in a conviction that women were only attracted to tall men, and consequently viewing himself as perpetually disadvantaged.

Before we started working together, John was not aware of his ability to choose his values. He fell into a vicious cycle of self-sabotage. As he spiraled into drama, his default response was to complain, assert that women were superficial, and blame them for his lack of success. It is tempting to play the Victim, and therefore it is important to remember that such behavior does not absolve you of your responsibility. You alone have the power to shape how you perceive, react to, and value your experiences. You are the architect of the standards by which you measure your life.

Beliefs divide us, values unite us, and the historical event that occurred in the early months of World War I is a powerful and poignant illustration of how our shared humanity can cut across even the most bitter of divides. British and German forces found themselves mired in the infamous trenches that stretched across Belgium, with their lives turning into a

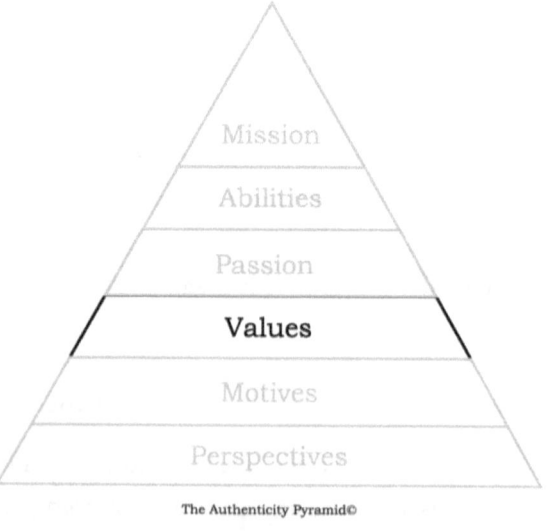

The Authenticity Pyramid©

relentless cycle of hardship, danger, and the crushing bleakness of war. With the added misery of a harsh winter, you could be forgiven for thinking that Christmas would have been a bleak affair that year. But something quite extraordinary happened on the eve of December 24, 1914. As the British soldiers hunkered down for the night, they heard an unexpected sound: the German troops singing Christmas carols. Their enemy had lined their trenches with lit Christmas trees, bringing a sliver of warmth and light to the cold, dark battlefield. The British soldiers, touched by this display of shared celebration, responded in kind with carols of their own.

Then, as the night deepened, something even more amazing happened. The German soldiers began to wish the British soldiers a Merry Christmas - in English, no less. They proposed a ceasefire for the holiday, a reprieve from the fighting. The British soldiers, initially cautious and fearing it was a trap, eventually emerged from their trenches. They found the German soldiers unarmed, holding out gifts of cigarettes and plum puddings as tokens of goodwill. For the next few days, they played soccer together, exchanged stories of home, and even held joint funeral services to honor their fallen comrades. The Christmas Truce of 1914, as it came to be known, was not an officially sanctioned event. It was a spontaneous act of humanity that rose above the cruel reality of war, emphasizing the soldiers' shared experiences over their roles as enemies. As the war intensified, these moments of shared humanity became less frequent, and even forbidden by the higher-ups.

This historical event beautifully illustrates the importance and power of our internal ethical compass. When you act against your values, it creates a feeling of guilt, and that is the signal that you have deviated from your core principles. This guilt serves as a catalyst for change and prompts you to make amends and adjust your decisions to align more closely with your values. However, sometimes, you might find yourself at odds with your proclaimed values, creating an internal conflict. For instance, you might claim to value ambition and hard work yet find yourself spending the whole day playing video games. This disconnects between what you say you value and what you actually do can possibly lead to self-deception, and causes a divide between your actions and your perceived identity.

Do you realize the power of value-driven decisions? The decisions you make, when grounded in your deeply held values, stir change, prompt action, and inspire others to do the same. This evokes a significant question for you: What changes can your value-driven decisions bring about in your life and those around you? If you have ever felt a nagging sense that something in your life just is not aligning, like there is a persistent discomfort or dissatisfaction with your choices, chances are you are experiencing a dissonance between your decisions and your values. Imagine you are playing a grand piano, and a few of the strings are slightly off-pitch—it might still sound mostly alright, but those discordant notes throw off the entire harmony. That is how it is with decisions that do not chime in with your values. They introduce dissonance into your life and create friction, stress, and unease. The beautiful symphony that is your life deserves to be in tune.

You might have established certain benchmarks for success and failure in your life, consciously or unconsciously. These might be influenced by societal standards, peer pressure, or parental expectations. However, these benchmarks are flexible and can be adjusted to better fit your personal needs and aspirations. When you experience negative emotions like stress, anxiety, or fear, it is often because you perceive a situation as threatening to your values, indicating a potential "failure." But if you scrutinize this situation more deeply, you might realize that the perceived threat does not match your true values. It is like fearing the loss of a toy that you do not really like - the fear does not make much sense, does it? In a similar vein, you might be pursuing certain goals because you think they align with your values, but upon closer examination, you might discover a disconnect. For instance, you might be chasing a high-paying job because you value financial stability, but at the same time, you are stressed, overworked, and do not have time for your loved ones. If you reassess your values, you might realize that you value quality time with your loved ones more than money. Once you identify this, you can make changes to realign your goals with your actual values, leading to a more fulfilled and balanced life.

Oh, how important it is to understand that your values are deeply intertwined with your identity and emotional responses! When something good happens to someone or something you value - say, your friend gets a new car, your spouse gets a raise, or your favorite team wins a championship - you feel elated, as though the event happened to you personally. Conversely, if something happens to a person or entity you do not value or even perceive as harmful, you might feel a sense of indifference or even satisfaction. Remember the scenes of jubilation on the streets when Osama Bin Laden was killed or when notorious serial killer Ted Bundy was executed? These reactions can be seen as a reflection of shared societal values.

What does this all mean for you? Well, this understanding of your values and aligning them with your actions guide you toward a more authentic, fulfilling life where your decisions and actions reflect who you truly are, and the person you aspire to be. Just like those soldiers on that chilly Christmas Eve in 1914, this understanding helps bridge divides and foster understanding, both within yourself and with others. As societies progress and individuals are presented with more freedom and opportunity for self-expression, there is an increased emphasis on values such as equality, responsibility, and transparency. In a world where you are often bombarded with information and choices, it is your values that help you navigate effectively through the distractions and external influences.

Living in alignment with your values is where integrity comes into play. When you act with integrity, your actions become the embodiment of your deepest principles, echoing consistency and trustworthiness. Think of integrity and authenticity as two sides of the same coin. Integrity focuses on the consistency between your values and actions, and authenticity is about being true to your unique self. This means embracing your strengths and weaknesses, your passions, and your quirks—every facet that makes you, well, you. When you are authentic, you let go of societal pressures or the need to please others. You refuse to wear masks or play roles that do not align with who you genuinely are. When you combine authenticity with integrity, you create a harmony that resonates with your soul consciousness, establishing a unified state of existence. This powerful combination provides you with a sense of purpose and direction. As you move forward, keep in mind that your purpose is not one that is handed to you, but one that you cultivate based on your perspectives, motives, and values. Your journey shapes it, the lessons you learn, the challenges you overcome, and the wisdom you gain.

You might initially think of values as simple labels or tags that describe what people, including you, find meaningful or important. Words like "integrity," "trust," "honesty," and "creativity" might pop into your mind when you think about values. This perspective aligns with how the Oxford Dictionary defines values, which it describes as *"one's judgment of what is essential in life."* But There is a lot more to values than just that. One person who has done a lot of thinking and research on this topic is Richard Barrett, an internationally recognized thought leader on the evolution of human values. His work spans over a quarter of a century and offers a much richer and more nuanced understanding of what human values are. According to Barrett, values are the driving forces behind our ambitions and goals. This definition of values ties in closely with your own personal journey of self-awareness. When you define your values, you gain a deeper insight into why you act the way you do, why certain things matter to you, and why you make certain decisions. For instance, if honesty is one of your core values, you might feel compelled to always tell the truth, even when it is difficult or uncomfortable. If creativity is a top value for you, you might find yourself constantly drawn toward new ideas and innovative ways of doing things.

Coming back to John, the client who felt that his dating life was a bust because he was too short, John was fixated on a singular value - height. Because of this limiting belief, he denied himself the possibility of finding genuine love and connection. His height, which he could not change, became his definition of success in dating. He never paused to ponder on his perception of success and failure. He simply assumed that his lack of height meant automatic failure in the dating world. Now, what if John had been brave enough to address his "why" questions? What if he had questioned why he considered height the ultimate criterion of attractiveness? Would he have realized that this value was misguided and distorted, setting him up for constant disappointment? Possibly. This is also linked to the ineffective diagnosis of what the real problem was.

If you are keen to define your values, grab a notebook and spend a few moments answering the questions in Exercise 8.3 in the Appendix section. You will also find a reference of the top values and the traits associated with them for your guidance. Take it as advice from me: Regularly question and examine your values, and ask yourself if your decisions align with your values. Are your values causing unnecessary stress and anxiety, or are they leading to fulfillment and happiness? I encourage you to not let a misalignment of values keep you from making decisions that give you genuine happiness and fulfillment. It is never too late to reassess your values and make changes to better align your decisions with your true self.

Chapter 9

The Empowering Possibility

Now that you have more clarity on who you are, it is time to become confident in what you are capable of. This chapter is all about harnessing the power of your individuality and recognizing the boundless potential that lies within you. If you want to make your life a place rich with possibilities, opportunities, and growth, you need to ensure that the decisions you make are building this life for you. To do so, make decisions that empower you to satisfy your passion, and gain confidence by depending on your abilities. These are the main two takeaways of this chapter.

Perhaps you have always had an inclination towards art but never gave yourself the chance to pick up a paintbrush, or maybe there is a particular cause that tugs at your heartstrings but you have hesitated to get involved. Now is the moment to dive into those passions and let them guide you towards making more fulfilling

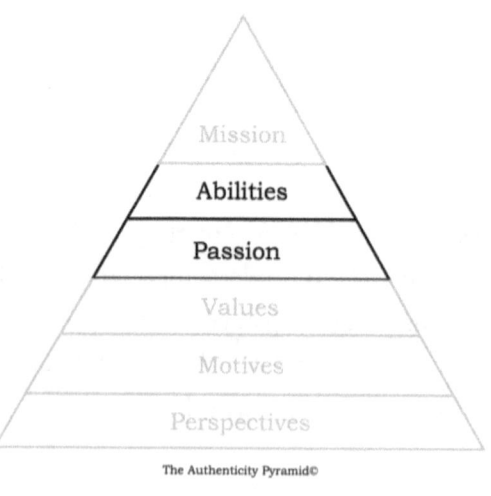

The Authenticity Pyramid©

decisions. When I mention assessing your abilities, I do not mean listing skills or qualifications on a resume. I mean the unique blend of talents and strengths you bring to the table as a person and a professional. Each of us has a distinctive set of capabilities that are shaped by personal traits, experiences, learnings, and innate talents. There is great value in preparing yourself to leverage them in the most fulfilling and impactful ways, especially when you are about to make big decisions.

Your Passions

I cannot speak about passion and not be passionate about it, and I am not shy to be so. A quick disclaimer here: I am a logical person myself, and to me passion-driven decisions used to sound fluff to me. Until I came across the stories of historical heroes who have turned the world upside down, and I understood that

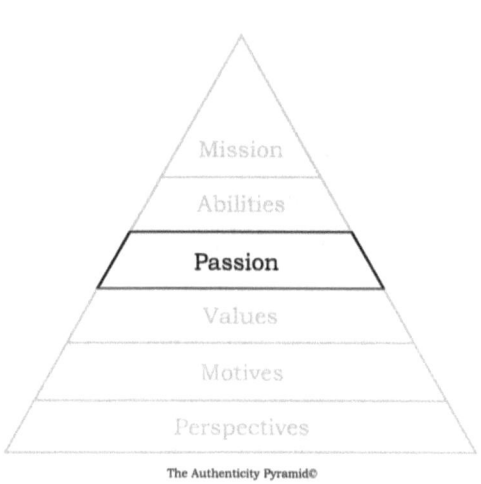

The Authenticity Pyramid©

passion is fluff when it is built on emotions only, but blossoms into an unstoppable force when built on vision and authentic motivation. I think of passion and immediately get mental pictures of a few of my heroes.

I think of Vincent Van Gogh pouring his heart out onto canvases, giving birth to Starry Night and Sunflowers, all despite his battle with mental illness. I think of Nikola Tesla, whose unwavering passion for uncovering nature's mysteries led to groundbreaking discoveries, forever transforming our understanding of electricity. Even in solitude, his heart echoed with the rhythm of scientific exploration. I think of passion, and the resilience of Anne Sullivan springs to my mind. Fueled by her passion for education, she broke through barriers to communicate with Helen Keller. Her unwavering commitment opened a new world for Keller and left an indelible mark on the field of special education. I remember the extraordinary journey of Ernest Shackleton, the British explorer whose passion for adventure led him to the uncharted icy landscapes of Antarctica. I visualize the tenacity of Billie Jean King being driven by a passion for equality and championing the rights of women in sports. I see Beethoven, almost entirely deaf, yet composing symphonies that would echo through the ages. I think of passion, and I see Julia Child captivated by the art of French cuisine and bringing its wonders to American households. I envision Marie Curie being driven by an insatiable curiosity and passion for science, eventually becoming the first woman to win a Nobel Prize and the only person to win it in two different scientific fields—physics and chemistry. I look at Steve Jobs, whose passion for innovation reshaped the landscape of technology.

Passion is a powerful force—It is that spark, that burning flame, that ignites within you and drives you to pursue what truly matters to you, often against all odds. When coupled with vision and an authentic motive, passion transforms from a simple emotion into a driving force. Consider the glorious examples I've shared with you—the legends, the pioneers, and the revolutionaries. Each of them was driven by an undeniable passion that permeated their very being and was transformed into an energy so profound that it propelled them toward their unique destinies. The outcomes they achieved were deeply intertwined with their passion for their fields and their causes. This passion was rooted in a deep understanding of themselves. For each of these individuals, their passion was connected to their innermost values, their aspirations, and their authentic selves, and this connection generated a profound clarity on how they decided to spend their lives.

But why does this clarity matter so much, especially when it comes to decision-making? Well, when you have a clear picture of what drives you, you automatically have clarity on what you want to do and you become more likely to make decisions that are congruent with this clarity. This congruence, in turn, leads you to increased satisfaction and success. And so, I consider recognizing your passions and connecting them to your authentic self to be a practical approach to adding a new layer of clarity to your decision-making. When you grasp what sets your heart aflame, you are more likely to make decisions that reflect these passions. This means choosing a career that aligns with your passion, opting for hobbies that stoke your inner fire, or even making lifestyle choices that mirror your deepest interests.

For instance, if you discover a deep-seated passion for nature, you may choose a career in environmental science, decide to live a more sustainable lifestyle or spend your free time volunteering at a local nature reserve. These decisions, stemming from your passion and your enhanced self-awareness, lead to a life that is more aligned with your true self and, in turn, is likely to bring you greater fulfillment and joy. In essence, discovering your passion and nurturing self-awareness equips you with the clarity needed for better decision-making.

One second, let me ask you a question: Do you sometimes feel jealous of those people out there running around all the time on Red Bulls and cannot wait to wake up in the morning because they are obsessed with an idea, and not sure why you do not have the same drive towards something specific? If yes, then I guess you will be happy to know that there is a scientific explanation to this. The sense of passion that you experience can be influenced by a variety of other factors, many of which are rooted in biology and psychology. Our objective now is to equip you with the knowledge and tools that will help you get back on your feet and revive this passion of yours. For this, I have some research to share and a few exercises will help. By the end of this next section, you will have clarity on what you are truly passionate about.

Firstly, passion could be genetic. The case of the Bach family illustrates a fascinating blend of genetic and environmental influences on passion, notably in music. This intertwining can be traced to genes like the dopamine D4 receptor gene linked with novelty-seeking behaviors, and leads to a tendency to develop strong passions. It is more like a recipe where genes (the ingredients) interact with each other and the environment (the cooking method). In the Bach family's case, their genetic predisposition likely mingled with their musically rich environment, resulting in a shared passion for music. You see, your love for something like painting might stem from both genetic predisposition and exposure to art at a young age. The key takeaway is that you are a complex blend of nature and nurture; your passions are influenced by both genetic and environmental factors, but genetics don't predetermine them, and understanding this fosters reflection and openness toward discovering your passions. That being said, here's an exercise that could help you reflect on whether there might be some genetic influence in your passions. Grab your notebook and head to Exercise 9.1 in the Appendix section.

Passion is also biological. The human brain, with its extraordinary structure and function, is the driving force behind your passions, ambitions, and zest for life. These intricate neural pathways' main function is to transport information, and so become the bedrock of your interests. When you pursue a passion, several brain areas become animated like a pinball machine, and your limbic system, including the amygdala, hippocampus, and hypothalamus, regulates emotional responses, while the reward system releases dopamine, encouraging and rewarding you in your pursuit. Your brain's executive suite, the prefrontal cortex, gets creative and helps you focus to overcome obstacles. Your brain's ability to adapt through neuroplasticity means that continuous engagement in passionate activities strengthens neural pathways, refining skills and fueling your desire for more. A prime example of this is Albert Einstein's passion for physics, driven in part by these brain mechanics. Your brain's natural neuroplasticity might turn a spark of interest into intense passion, as evidenced by research from Concordia University on individuals with harmonious passion who reported higher levels of well-being. In simpler words, your brain is a passion-generating powerhouse, and you can channel this power into pursuits that bring joy, fulfillment, and purpose.

As a coach, I would develop two hypotheses if you tell me that you do not feel passionate about something at the moment:

1.   You are yet to discover what you are truly passionate about.
2.   You do have a passion, and a limiting belief hinders it.

You will find two exercises in the Appendix section, Exercises 9.2 for the first hypothesis, and 9.3 for the second. These two exercises are designed for you to self-coach yourself. If you still believe you need a deeper conversation, get in touch with me and we will work on exploring further what is slowing your brain's passion-generating activity.

Central to understanding passion is the Self-Determination theory, which outlines three psychological needs: autonomy, competence, and relatedness. If you have the freedom to choose, feel skilled at what you do, and connect with others, you are likely to experience motivation and passion and find the courage to make more authentic decisions. For instance, if you are a software developer with the freedom to choose projects, confidence in skills, and strong bonds with a team, your passion will be automatically fueled, and you will find yourself in what you can call a 'Flow State'. The 'Flow State', coined by psychologist Mihaly Csikszentmihalyi, is that absorbing mental state where time vanishes, and you are completely engrossed in an activity.

If you do not have a problem finding your passion because you already have, know that -beside the genetic and biological reasons- your unique personality traits also shape your passions. A curious individual might be passionate about traveling or learning languages, while a more introspective person might find joy in writing or seeking knowledge. Your passions reflect your inner self, as evidenced by the rise of passion-driven careers and entrepreneurs like Elon Musk. It is incredible how your mind's complexities can fuel your passions and light the way forward. If you are still exploring what motivates you, you might want to revisit previous sections of The Authenticity Pyramid© on motives to discover what truly ignites your passion.

Also, the origins of your passion might be formed by external influences. If you adore books, would your passion for reading feel the same if you were born in a society where books were considered obsolete, replaced by holograms or audio narratives? Probably not; your passion might lean more toward the technology behind these replacements. Your environment has a significant role in shaping your passions. If you are brought up in a bustling city with towering skyscrapers, you might develop a love for urban design or finance. Conversely, growing up in the tranquil countryside might lead you toward a passion for agriculture or stargazing. It is not a rule, more of one more reason for you to explore the origins of what you find yourself passionate about, and further test if this passion is authentic, or influenced. Think about what you love and trace its origin, understand if it aligns with your personal values or society's expectations, and examine how it makes you feel deep inside. True passion should energize you and make you lose track of time. If it stresses you, it might be a product of societal pressures or made-beliefs. Identifying the source of your passion is not meant to diminish its value, but rather to enhance your understanding and appreciation of it. Whether it resonates with personal, societal, or cultural aspects, what is essential and truly matters is that it brings joy and adds value to your life. Ultimately, the nature of passion is complex and multifaceted, influenced by a blend of our inherent traits, experiences, environments, and external circumstances. It is an ongoing journey of self-discovery and growth, and like any journey, it comes with its twists and turns. If you want to examine further whether your passion is authentic or influenced, and you need more than the simple framework I shared above, Exercise 9.4 in the Appendix section is designed for you.

In a nutshell, the interplay between individual inclinations and external influences takes center stage. Imagine the moment when a young child, playing with colorful building blocks discovers a fascination for architecture, or when an accidental meeting with a local artist turns into a lifelong passion for painting. These sparks of interest grow into defining aspects of your professional and personal life. They shape your decisions and guide you toward choices that resonate with your inner self. The alignment between passion and decision-making is grounded in cognitive psychology and neuroscience. Your brain's reward systems get activated when engaging with interests you love and reinforces positive behavior, driving you toward success in those areas. Whether it is the joy of cooking for others or the thrill of solving complex mathematical problems, realizing your passions empowers you to create a roadmap for decision-making that is both fulfilling and aligned with your true self.

Your Abilities

One of my clients, we will call her Sarah, is a young professional stuck at a crossroads in her career. She was an accountant by trade but discovered a passion for painting, a talent for calming tense situations among her friends, and an uncanny ability to decode the emotions of those around her. She had an opportunity to shift into art therapy, a field that seemingly blended her unique abilities. The problem was that she was unsure if she was ready to make this decision. When she took a step back and recognized the varied bits of intelligence she possessed, from Logical-Mathematical to Interpersonal, she got the confidence to switch careers and actually excelled in a role that harmonized her unique blend of skills. Within two years, Sarah's practice thrived, and her clients often remarked on how her multifaceted approach made a difference in their lives. Sarah found what she wanted to do and is living confidently and joyfully. What gave her the confidence to make this decision is the confidence she had in her ability to perform exceptionally and overcome all potential challenges that might face her after making this decision. She knew 'she had it'. This is what I mean by *abilities*.

In the movie 'Good Will Hunting,' you watch as Matt Damon's character, Will Hunting, a humble janitor at MIT, stumbles upon a daunting math problem etched on a blackboard outside a professor's office. Despite his status as a janitor and not a student, Will cracks the puzzle anonymously with ease. The scene repeats with an even more complex problem, and once again, Will solves it. This time, he is caught red-handed by the professor, who stands speechless as he gazes at the correctly solved problem on the blackboard. This might sound like a far-fetched Hollywood plot, but it is, in fact, inspired by the real-life story of the renowned mathematician George Bernard Dantzig.

Dantzig was a prominent mathematician acclaimed for developing the simplex algorithm, a key tool in linear programming. It is used widely to optimize solutions to problems defined by linear mathematics, whether that is maximizing profits, minimizing losses, or planning the most cost-effective diet for an army. One of the stepping stones that led him to these significant contributions was a chance occurrence during his student life. While Dantzig was studying statistics under Professor Jerzy Neyman at UC Berkeley, he turned up late to a class and found two problems chalked up on the blackboard, which he mistook for homework. He noted them down and realized they were tougher than the usual fare. Fast forward a few weeks, Neyman, bursting with excitement, turns up at Dantzig's house, holding a paper introduced as "one of your papers", urging him to get it ready for publication. Neyman explained that the 'homework problems' were, in fact, two unsolved statistical problems of great renown, and suggested that Dantzig compile the two solutions and present them as his thesis. Time passed, and Dantzig became an esteemed computer scientist and mathematician.

Dantzig's story was already making waves as a testament to the power of positive thinking before it made its way into Hollywood. A Lutheran televangelist from Los Angeles broadcasted a slightly exaggerated version, claiming that even Einstein couldn't solve the problems that Dantzig tackled and that his professor instantly offered him a job when he saw the correct solutions. Despite the theatrical touch, the core message remained – the power of unknowingly facing a seemingly impossible challenge with a can-do attitude. Dantzig himself said once, "If I had known that the problems were not homework but two famous unsolved problems in statistics, I probably would not have approached them positively, become discouraged, and never solved them."

I have another story to share that was published in the Local Business Journal in 2020, about a young man, Thomas, an unassuming manager in a small manufacturing company. Thomas was facing a complex decision requiring skills beyond his known capabilities. He was tasked with implementing a new, technologically advanced system to streamline operations, and immediately realized he lacked the technological expertise to make an informed decision. Thomas decided to invest in expanding his abilities, refusing to give in to thoughts of "this is not for me" or "I am not qualified for this job." Instead, he committed to a series of workshops, online tutorials, and mentorship sessions to understand the technologies he was evaluating. The more he learned, the more his confidence grew. Thomas's newfound confidence came from a deeper understanding of his ability to learn, adapt, and grow. His confidence was in knowing that he had the capacity to become competent in a previously unfamiliar area.

Inside of him, he became aware of his resilience and willpower to face and overcome challenges, even if they seemed intimidating at first.

This, my friend, is where confidence comes from. Actually, this resonates strongly with the work of psychologist Daniel Goleman on emotional intelligence, who asserts that self-awareness and self-confidence are integral to decision-making. Similarly, psychologist Gary Klein's published research in 1998 on decision-making underscores the importance of

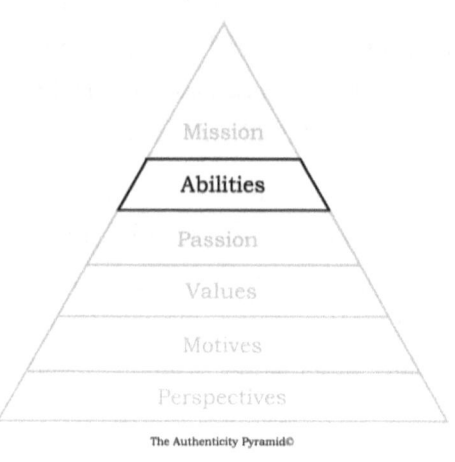

The Authenticity Pyramid©

experience and intuition cultivated through practice and learning. And so, back to Thomas, it was his commitment to expanding his skills that helped him form an intuitive understanding of the complex technologies involved. The outcome? Thomas had the clarity and confidence to make an informed decision that revolutionized the company's operational efficiency. The process he followed of recognizing a lack in his skillset, deciding to expand his abilities, and gaining the confidence to make the complex decision he had to make, is exactly what I am trying to tell you here.

In your world, you might be presented with a challenging project that others hesitate to take on. Self-confidence is knowing that whatever challenges may arise, you do have the mental and emotional strength to take them on and win over them. Your confidence in your skills should be grounded in real experiences and past successes, and this encourages you to make the bold decision to lead the project. Even when unexpected problems arise, your belief in your capabilities empowers you to navigate them rather than becoming paralyzed by doubt or fear. When it comes to personal growth and relationships, knowing what you are capable of is not only about skills and expertise; it is also about emotional intelligence and self-awareness.

Let us say you have a passion for languages and have successfully learned a new language before, and now considering taking up another one. Others might see it as a daunting task, but your awareness of your learning methods, discipline, and previous success fuels your decision to pursue it. Others do not have this awareness, and their doubt in themselves is where the naysaying comes from. You know the journey will be filled with complexities, but your confidence in your capability guides you through. When it comes to managing bias, realizing what you are capable of also means recognizing where biases might cloud your judgment. For example, you might be an excellent financial analyst, but your close relationship with a friend who is starting a business might lead to an overestimation of the venture's success. Recognizing this potential bias, you can take a step back, evaluate the situation objectively, and make a decision based on your analytical skills rather than personal feelings.

In these scenarios and more, knowing what you are capable of acts as a confidence station. It directs your decisions and protects you from undue doubt or external pressures. When you align your decisions with a profound awareness of your abilities, you directly empower yourself to face the consequences and unforeseen challenges with resilience and grace. This is your brain's way of saying, "I've got this", and indeed, you do. And so, when you invest time in expanding your abilities and learning new skills, you lead yourself to an increase in confidence, which in turn affects the way you make decisions. Learning a new programming language, for example, does not only increase your efficiency in the workplace. Your confidence grows as you master it, enabling you to contribute ideas more freely, communicate more effectively with your team, and make decisions more confidently. A study by the Harvard Business Review in 2015 found that employees who actively sought out learning opportunities were 47% more likely to be engaged in their work, leading to better decision-making and innovation within the organization. In your personal life, this could translate into pursuing a hobby like gardening, photography, or cooking. The joy you find in nurturing a plant, capturing a perfect shot, or creating a delicious meal is an experience that builds your confidence and empowers you to approach other aspects of life with greater assurance and clarity. The real magic happens when you begin to see how these expanded abilities intertwine with your daily life, leading you to make decisions that are not only better but also more aligned with who you truly are.

One of the most effective and scientific ways to figure out your edge, and accordingly make many important decisions including your career projection and personal relationships, is to be aware of your natural intelligence. I am not talking about an IQ test; being intelligent means more than just the ability to analyze and solve complex problems. Howard Gardner, an American developmental psychologist, proposed the theory of multiple intelligences in his book "Frames of Mind: The Theory of Multiple Intelligences." He suggested that traditional measures of intelligence, which mainly focus on linguistic and logical-mathematical abilities, are too narrow.

Gardner argued for the existence of at least eight different types of intelligence, such as musical intelligence, spatial intelligence, interpersonal intelligence, and naturalist intelligence, among others. Gardner's Multiple Intelligence Theory paints a rich and detailed panorama of your abilities. It highlights how various types of intelligence work together, shaping not only your life but also your career path.

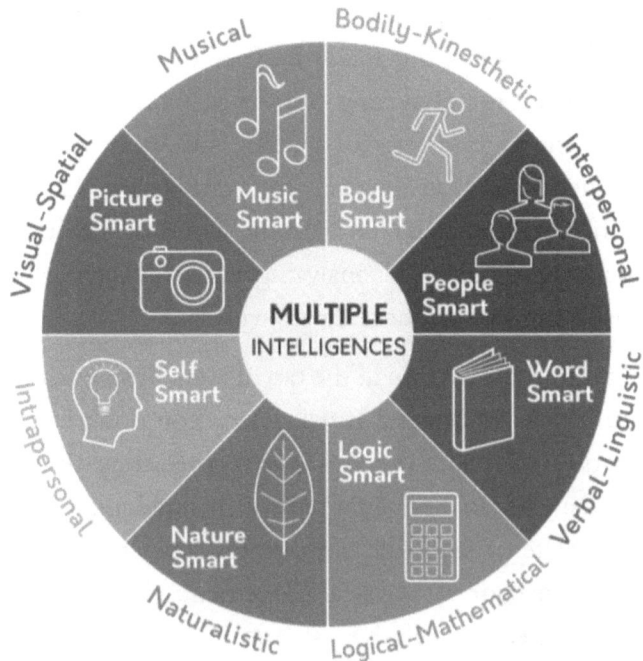

Historical figures like Mozart, known for his extraordinary musical intelligence, or Albert Einstein, celebrated for his logical-mathematical intelligence, exemplify the diversity of these intelligences. Similarly, today's innovators like Steve Jobs demonstrate the power of spatial intelligence in imagining and creating groundbreaking products.

If you find yourself sketching dream homes or envisioning complex structures, you may share being Visually Intelligent with architects like Frank Gehry. This ability to visualize and form mental models, known as Spatial Intelligence, is not confined to architecture. Surgeons like Dr. Ben Carson exhibit this intelligence in maneuvering through the human body. Imagine, your ability to map out your next family road trip might just be a spark of this intelligence. If you find joy in playing with words, crafting compelling narratives, or simplifying intricate concepts like authors J.K. Rowling and Stephen King, you are tapping into Linguistic Intelligence. This form is about the articulate arguments crafted by lawyers such as

Amal Clooney. If you excel at writing heartfelt emails or persuading friends with your words, this might be your form of intelligence. Should you have a knack for dissecting problems, understanding patterns, or perhaps enjoying a good Sudoku puzzle, you are probably delving into Logical-Mathematical Intelligence. Innovators like Elon Musk have leveraged this intelligence to navigate the world of tech business. If you are someone who thrives in analyzing and solving problems in your professional setup, this might resonate with you.

If you can feel the rhythm in the tap of a raindrop or can create catchy jingles, you may have Musical Intelligence. You don't have to be Alicia Keys to harness this intelligence; even appreciating the rhythm-based language in daily life makes you a part of this melodious world. Perhaps you are an athlete or someone who simply loves to dance in the living room. This connection to physical movement, visible in champions like Lionel Messi, reflects Bodily-Kinesthetic Intelligence. Even your knack for creating artistic DIY projects could be an expression of this form. If you are passionate about gardening, cooking, or simply enjoy nature walks, you may possess Naturalist Intelligence. Chefs like Jamie Oliver utilize this intelligence to create culinary masterpieces. Your ability to differentiate between spices or enjoy the subtle beauty of nature might just connect you to this form.

Do you find joy in philosophical debates or pondering life's big questions? You might be navigating the realm of Existential Intelligence, much like the Dalai Lama. Your curiosity about the meaning of life and spirituality may be a sign of this profound intelligence. Your ability to empathize with friends or lead a team at work could be a manifestation of Interpersonal Intelligence. Empathetic leaders like Nelson Mandela have used this intelligence to bring about significant social change. If you excel at understanding others and building connections, this might be your form. Lastly, the introspective world of Intrapersonal Intelligence may speak to you if you have a deep understanding of your emotions, strengths, and weaknesses. Oprah Winfrey harnessed this intelligence for her success. If you often reflect on your feelings and desires, you may find resonance here.

One of my clients, we will call him Tim, has always been drawn to understanding the emotions and motivations of those around him. He possesses an innate ability to empathize, listen, and provide support. After losing his best friend to a battle with mental illness, he was driven to make a life-changing decision inspired by his natural talents and his personal experience. He decided to become a mental health counselor. He acknowledged his intrinsic ability to connect with people and realized how this skill could be used to make a real difference in the lives of those struggling with mental health. He aligned his career path with his inner strengths, and made a decision that does not just influence his life but also the lives of those he will help in the future. Another client, we will call him Mark, is a successful corporate executive who feels an unexplained connection to nature. His weekends are spent hiking and exploring, and he feels a profound sense of fulfillment in these activities. A turning point comes when he volunteers for a local environmental protection group and realizes his passion and talent for conservation. Despite a lucrative career, Mark makes the bold decision to shift to environmental policy. It is a decision driven by self-awareness, an understanding of his talents, and a desire to align his professional life with what he feels to be his true calling. In relationships, too, recognizing one's abilities does lead to significant life decisions. A couple might discover their mutual talent in understanding and nurturing children, and this realization leads them to become foster parents, a profound and life-altering decision that brings a new sense of purpose to their lives.

The science behind these decisions is rooted in positive psychology and the understanding of personal strengths. I agree with Dr. Martin Seligman when he stated that recognizing and utilizing personal strengths is associated with greater well-being and satisfaction in life. When you align your significant life decisions with your inherent talents, you are embracing a journey that resonates with who you truly are and what you are capable of. When you know what you are passionate about and combine it with what you are naturally good, you are empowered to make decisions that don't just affect your life's trajectory but also impact those around you in meaningful ways. Whether in your career, relationships, or personal development, recognizing your talents is the compass guiding you to make decisions that are deeply fulfilling. Like Sarah, Mark, and the couple who chose to foster children, your talents are the key to unlocking new possibilities and the driver behind making bold and confident decisions.

If you are already super clear on what it is that you do better than anyone else and always receive positive feedback, skip the following exercise and go directly to the next chapter to learn how to set a mission for your life. If, on the other hand, you find your career and relationships not as exciting as you wish them to be and are unable to find the uniqueness about you in them, then let me tell you that there are two ways of doing this. There is the easy and shortcut way and another deeper and more authentic way. If you want to truly discover your talents, I hope you understand that a free online assessment is not enough. There are loads of free online assessments, and I can recommend a few if you get in touch (just send an email to *info@ivicdecisions.com*, and we will send you a bunch of those). If, however, you combine the passion exercises in the previous chapter with Exercise 9.5 in the Appendix section, you are more likely to achieve results that keep you going for a lifetime.

Chapter 10

The Relevant Possibility

Moving on to the next pillar in the IVIC Decision-Making Framework©, Vision, the following step involves filtering out possibilities that do not necessarily help you achieve what you want, namely, your life's mission. You know that humble piece of iron that costs just about

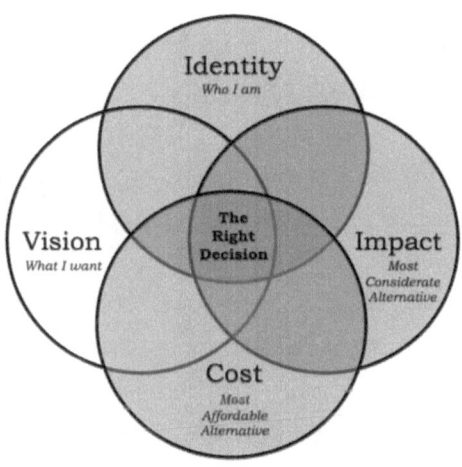

IVIC Decision-Making Framework©

$100 to buy? If you take that iron bar and craft it into horseshoes, the value leaps up to around $250. If you shape it into sewing needles instead, hold on to your hat because the value skyrockets to an impressive $70,000! But if you dig deeper into the creative toolbox and decide to produce delicate watch springs, the value ascends to a staggering $6 million! The point I am trying to make is that your worth is not simply what you are made of, whether it is high intelligence or multiple positive personality traits. Instead, it is largely about the multitude of ways in which you can maximize your innate abilities and resources, and the real value you bring to life's table.

You and I need to achieve a common understanding of how a belief system works before we address setting a mission for your life. The estimated number of different religions and worldviews is 4,300. Statistically speaking, the chances that you and I have different ways of looking at life and finding meaning in it is more than the chances of them being similar. The common understanding you and I need to reach, however, is more of a value than a belief.

As I mentioned before, beliefs separate us, but values do bring us together, and I will appreciate it if both of us embrace the values of authenticity, integrity, and curiosity as we go through this argument together. At the end of the day, my role as an author and coach is not to try and convince you with a specific worldview. All I am doing is bringing your attention to facts and perspective, and then encouraging you to make sense out of them on your own. If you have been embracing a growth mindset throughout this reading experience, chances are you already have started thinking about a few things differently, and maybe even changed your mind when it comes to some realizations. If you read throughout the rest of your chapter with curiosity, you are more likely to acknowledge that realizing your blind spots is not an admission of failure or a stain on your intelligence. It is akin to realizing that your life has more chapters yet to be written, and that there is still more for you to explore and understand about yourself. If you have ever felt like you have mastered a subject only to discover a whole new layer of complexity, you know that the world's dynamic and evolving nature keeps us on our toes.

Just like believing you have mastered cooking after trying one recipe would be ludicrous, thinking you have all the answers after a glimpse of knowledge can be equally misleading. It might feel comfortable, especially in areas of life where beliefs are more rigid, such as in some

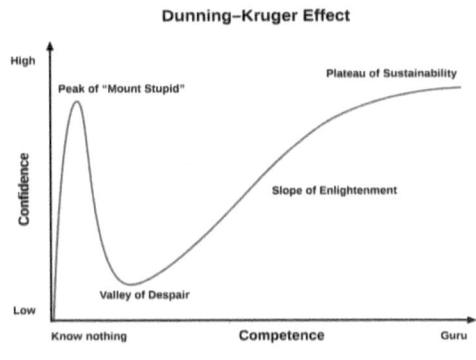

religious or political contexts. But this comfort can lead to stagnation, and as physicist Stephen Hawking wisely observed, "The greatest enemy of knowledge is not ignorance; it is the illusion of knowledge." If you are a student, professional, or anyone passionate about learning, you will know that recognizing your blind spots is like finding the key to a library and opening up worlds of knowledge. A psychological phenomenon called the Dunning-Kruger effect illustrates this point, where those with limited ability in a task may overestimate their ability, while those more competent may underestimate themselves.

If you want to expand your horizons, you need to cultivate curiosity and an eagerness to learn. In your professional life, this might mean attending workshops, reading widely, or seeking mentors. In your personal life, it could be as simple as exploring a new hobby or engaging in meaningful conversations. And so, acknowledging that you do not have all the answers and that you still have more to learn is the beginning of growth. Stephen Hawking cautioned us against genuine ignorance. His words resonate with me today, and I hope they resonate with you too, in a way that urges you toward learning and growth. So, if you are an engineer, a teacher, an artist, or anyone with a hunger for understanding, take a moment to embrace curiosity and question your preconceived notions.

Now, to the real discussion. Have the questions "Why am I here?" and "What is my purpose?" ever crossed your mind? Have you perceived them to be philosophical riddles or the keys to living a life that is *meaningful,* *fulfilling,* and *enlightening?* I am not planning to waste your time on fluffy or philosophical arguments; these

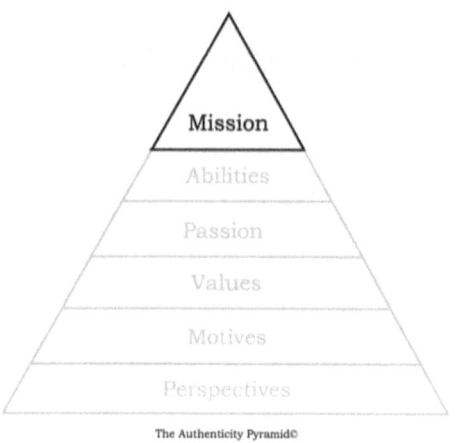

The Authenticity Pyramid©

three keywords do apply to my own life. I meet so many people every day in my capacity as a coach and trainer. I meet who they are inside, and I do understand the pain of living a life that is not *meaningful, fulfilling,* and *enlightening.* Some of them give up and claim that life is meaningless. Well, my friend, I will not tell you if your life is meaningful or not. This is a personal decision left to you, and only you, to make.

Let us play a little game that will help me illustrate my point, and you to understand what I am aiming at. Look around you, and count ten items in your space. This includes literally anything your eyes fall on. Done? Awesome. Now, for each of the items, ask yourself, "Why does this item exist?". For example, a cup is to hold liquid in it, a pen is to write, a bird is to protect the grass from worms, etc. Next, for each of the items, ask yourself, "Who is the main beneficiary of this item?" This will be the other thing that this item fulfills the need for. For example, a cup's beneficiary is the liquid, a pen's beneficiary is paper, a bird's beneficiary is the grass, etc. Now, it is your turn to ask yourself these two questions: "Why do you exist?", and "Who is your main beneficiary?"

Purpose is defined as the reason or impact a being exists for. It is the "why" of this being. A mission is the role or function that this being does to fulfill the reason and achieve the impact. It is the "what" of this being.

Recognizing your personal mission has real, practical implications for your everyday decisions. Imagine you are a scientist exploring the universe or the intricate details of a single cell. The same way, gravity and other physical laws are fine-tuned to allow for life, finding your own personal "fine-tuning" or purpose guides you in making complex choices. It is like having a compass that always points you in the right direction, whether you are choosing a career, building relationships, or setting personal goals. Shift your gaze to nature, where -for example- you are an ecologist. Just as bees have their purpose in pollinating plants, you, too, have a unique role to play. When you understand your purpose, decisions that might have seemed overwhelming become manageable and more evident. Your mission is like the roots of a tree that ground you and provide stability as you grow and branch out in different directions.

The philosophical side is equally illuminating. Victor Frankl's idea that the purpose of life is found in every moment of living underscores that clarity in your mission can transform even mundane choices into profound opportunities for growth. Knowing your purpose is akin to having a personalized roadmap, enabling you to navigate life's twists and turns with confidence. Even theological and cosmological perspectives have a part to play here. Whether you see life's purpose as divinely guided or part of a grand cosmic puzzle, understanding your place in it provides a sense of coherence and direction. It is like having a well-crafted script in a complex play; you know your lines and cues, and you can perform with assurance. So, back to you, pondering these profound questions of "Why?" and "What?". Setting a mission for your life provides a status that shapes your decisions, and provides you clarity and confidence while making them. This is the difference between wandering aimlessly, and moving forward with clarity and resolve. Whether it is a major life decision or a daily choice, knowing your purpose acts as a guiding star, leading you to fulfillment and success.

Here is a thought for you: You are designed to make a difference. Whether you think there is a superior force that has intentionally designed you this way or that you are a random product of nature is not the point here. Like bees and gravity, you are a unique and valuable part of an ecosystem, and knowing your mission enriches your decisions, adds meaning to your actions, and empowers you to contribute positively to the world around you. Next time you are in your garden or at your busy workplace, take a moment to reflect on how you are a piece of a beautiful puzzle with your very own purpose, and you will get what I mean. You do not have to worry about where this purpose is coming from; just decide on one for yourself, for your own sake.

What is the purpose of having a purpose, I hear you ask? Well, it is a fascinating idea, isn't it, that merely having a purpose in life could potentially prolong your existence? A study led by Patrick Hill, an assistant psychology professor at Carleton University in Ottawa, Canada, delved into the potential impact of a sense of life purpose on aging and adult development. Hill and his team analyzed data from the Midlife in the United States (MIDUS) study, sponsored by the National Institute on Aging, which gathered responses from over 6,000 people. A bit like opening a Pandora's box, this research uncovered remarkable insights. They found that fourteen years after the MIDUS study, those who expressed a stronger sense of purpose in life were more likely to outlive their peers. The stats are indeed startling. Having a purpose in life reduces the risk of death by 15%, regardless of when the person found their life direction—be it in their 20s, 50s, or 70s. This is pretty noteworthy when you consider that Hill's analysis controlled for other factors known to influence longevity, like age, gender, and emotional well-being.

Now, the concept of "purpose" is a broad one, much like an umbrella sheltering myriad possibilities. Hill describes it as something like a "compass or lighthouse that provides an overarching aim and direction in daily life." But this can mean different things for different people—it could be your passion for writing, your drive to help your community, or your commitment to your career. What is important is that it guides your decisions and brings meaning to your daily life. Hill's research suggests that having a purpose might boost health since those with a defined purpose are more likely to adopt healthier lifestyles.

But there is another potential advantage—it might help buffer the detrimental effects of stress. Another intriguing experiment, this one led by Anthony Burrow, a developmental psychologist at Cornell University, answers the question. He invited a diverse group of college student volunteers to ride rapid transit across various neighborhoods in Chicago. The students documented their emotional responses as the ethnic makeup of the passengers changed. The students were divided into two groups. Half of them wrote about their life purpose for about ten minutes, while the other half wrote about the last movie they had watched. The results were telling. Students who had pondered their purpose reported no increased stress as the ethnic diversity of the passengers changed, unlike their movie-pondering counterparts. While more research is certainly needed, these findings suggest that having a sense of purpose could serve as a sort of emotional shield, protecting us from stress and its potential consequences, such as an elevated risk of heart disease. The benefits of having a purpose seem to extend beyond just reducing stress. A large-scale U.S. study found that people who reported a higher sense of purpose in life had a 15% lower risk of death, regardless of whether they were retired or not. These findings suggest a powerful link between self-worth, a sense of purpose, and longevity.

To further reflect on how having a clear purpose positively impacts one's life, let us put a pause on scientific research and take a quick detour to Japan to explore the Japanese' philosophical concept of ikigai. Ikigai, roughly translating to "reason for being" in English, is a philosophy suggesting that everyone carries a unique sense of

purpose within them. The people of Okinawa, the island boasting the highest population of centenarians worldwide, attribute their longevity to a clear sense of ikigai. They believe it to be what wakes them up every day, offering fulfillment, joy, and significance to their lives. Japanese culture presents an interesting perspective on aging, especially when compared to the West. Many Japanese people continue to pursue their ikigai long past the traditional age of retirement. In fact, there is not a precise equivalent in the Japanese language for the English word "retirement," implying a permanent departure from the workforce. It seems that having a sense of purpose is so ingrained in their culture that the Western concept of retirement simply does not apply. This perspective, backed by research from longevity studies, emphasizes the role of a strong sense of community and a clearly defined ikigai, in addition to the well-known healthy Japanese diet, in promoting longevity.

If we look closer into the lives of Okinawans and other centenarians from "Blue Zones"—regions known for their exceptionally long-living populations—we find a few striking commonalities:

- They live longer than the average global citizen.
- They suffer less from chronic diseases like cancer and heart disease.

- Many display astounding vitality and health, exceeding what we would typically associate with their advanced years.
- Blood tests often show lower levels of free radicals, which cause cellular aging, due to their healthy diet and lifestyle habits.
- Both men and women maintain higher levels of sexual hormones later in life.
- Dementia rates are significantly below the global average.

What is the takeaway here? These findings suggest that having a strong sense of purpose, like the Japanese concept of ikigai, may not only enrich your life but also extend it. It is a compelling reason, is not it, to take some time for introspection and find your personal ikigai?

It is about time that I tell you how understanding what a purpose is changed how I define self-confidence. For context, I have spent the better part of my youth zigzagging across the globe, responding to cries for help wherever they were loudest. I have been all over the Middle East, Africa, and Asia, spending a decade of my life lending a hand to those who needed it across 20 countries in 3 continents. In 2015, my mission to support unfortunate people led me to the beautiful, earthquake-stricken, country of Nepal. I set off -with a heart heavy with sorrow for the devastating Gorkha earthquake's victims- on a mission to provide assistance to the thousands of people whose lives had been upturned by this natural disaster. I was compelled by the belief that my purpose directs me to extend a helping hand to those in immediate distress. There, I crossed paths with a young man who offered me to go visit him at Lumbini. Lumbini is renowned for its many monasteries and temples built on hallowed ground, and it was there that I met a Buddhist monk whose wisdom altered my perception of purpose and self-confidence. Our conversation unfolded over several hours, and I found myself captivated by the wisdom of his answers to my endless stream of philosophical questions. One question that particularly puzzled me was how to strike a balance between confidence and humility. I asked the monk, and in response, he invited me to look at the sun. He asked, with a perpetual smile that stayed on his face during our discourse, "What would you think if the sun proclaimed, 'Without me, everything dies?'". I instantly replied, "Arrogant, of course.". "Why?", he asked, and then explained "It is telling the truth. The sun is arrogant if it claims that it is the *only* source of life". The sun would be arrogant if it claimed that it is the *only* source of life, but realizing its role in the ecosystem is in essence realizing its value and importance, and thus providing it with the confidence to claim its role in life. It is then I understood the difference.

My conversation with the monk mirrors scientific evidence suggesting a strong correlation between a sense of purpose and self-esteem. A 2009 study published in the Journal of Research in Personality indicated a strong association between life purpose and self-esteem among 746 participants. Those with a clearer understanding of their life purpose reported higher self-esteem levels. The study's findings were echoed in another study published in Applied Psychology: Health and Well-being in 2011, involving over 7,000 American adults. Those reporting a higher sense of purpose also reported better physical health, economic success, and improved social relationships. From a neurological standpoint, these reports can be linked to the activation of certain brain areas associated with reward and motivation, like the ventral striatum and ventromedial prefrontal cortex. This stimulation fortifies the notion that if your life holds value and meaning, it will ultimately boost your self-worth.

Philosophically, the bond between self-confidence and life purpose is a notion that is central to various philosophical schools. Existentialists like Jean-Paul Sartre and Viktor Frankl advocate that individuals must create their own life purpose, which subsequently magnifies self-worth. This is seen as a manifestation of personal control over the direction of one's life. Eastern philosophy, particularly Buddhism, also envisions the concept of dharma, or life's purpose, as a key element of self-worth. Fulfilling one's dharma signifies a harmony between individual actions and the cosmic order, leading to an enriched sense of self-worth. The Stoics also propagated this link; they derived purpose from living in consonance with nature and reason, which induced inner peace and a firm sense of self-worth. Even Abrahamic religions acknowledge that there is a divine purpose behind every person's existence.

Reflecting on this captivating interaction with science and philosophy, and the lessons I learned myself from many life-changing situations and near-death experiences, I cannot help but see the profound impact of having a purpose and a clear life mission had on my life, and the clarity and confidence this has given me to make complex decisions look easy and impulsive. From all of these arguments and insights, I wish that you join me in acknowledging the relationship between purpose and confidence.

How do you set a mission, then? Think of yourself as a radio station broadcasting at a certain frequency. The messages and music you send out attract a specific audience. If you want to change your audience, you have to change your frequency, send out different messages, and play different music. Unlike words, which can be deceptive, energy is straightforward and uncompromising. As human beings, we are primarily beings of energy, constantly receiving and giving out energy. This is why you instantly feel drawn to or repelled by someone; because everything, including us, is made of energy and frequencies. You naturally gravitate toward frequencies that match your own. The movies, books, hobbies, and animals you are attracted to represent energy vibrating on a frequency that matches yours.

If -in reflection on the life purpose argument- your mind has taken you to conclusions like, "My purpose is to be happy" or "My mission is to be rich", know that what you are thinking about are life goals, not purpose. If you remember from our exercise earlier (with the 10 items and their purposes), everything that exists has a purpose for *something else* to prosper. A bottle of water does not exist to drink; it exists so that *you* drink. Grass does not exist to eat itself; it exists so that animals eat it. Air does not exist to breathe but for living beings to be able to breathe. You do not exist for yourself; you exist to fulfill a need that is outside of yourself, be it toward other humans, nature, or both.

If you are asking this question, it means you are ready to start setting a purpose for your life. The figure you see on the right is how the Japanese like to look at it. Briefly, you are able to find your purpose (Ikigai) by discovering a mission that succeeds in intersecting what you love, what you are good at, what you can make a living out of, and what the world needs. Exercise 10.1 will help you figure your life's mission out. Combine the findings of this exercise, along with the rest of the exercises covering other layers of The Authenticity Pyramid©, and -trust me on this one- the mission you will set for yourself will give you an unprecedented sense of clarity, confidence, and joy, and making complex decision will much easier. And, as always, I am available to chat if your experience finding your mission is not as smooth as you wish it to be. All you need to do is reach out to info@ivicdecisions.com and request a coaching conversation, and I promise to help you reach the clarity and confidence you seek.

Chapter 11

The Impactful Possibility

This is the story of what is arguably considered to be the most famous 'No' in modern history. On December 1st, 1955, Rosa Parks' day began like any other, working diligently as a seamstress before boarding the city bus to go home in Montgomery, Alabama. Back then, the rigid and unfair rules of the time were clear: White passengers sit at the front of the

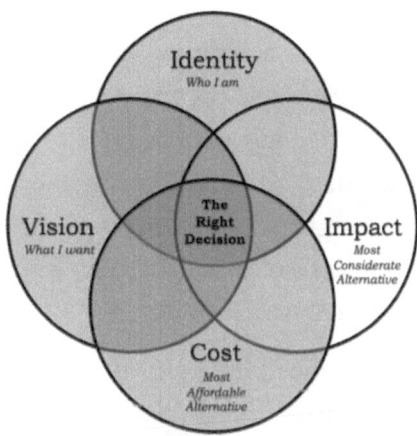

IVIC Decision-Making Framework©

bus, while Black passengers must sit at the back. As the bus filled up with passengers, the driver ordered Parks and three other Black passengers to vacate their seats for white passengers.

At this pivotal moment, Rosa Parks had to make a decision. She had two options: conform and reinforce a system that reduced her humanity, or resist and potentially face arrest, societal backlash, and personal danger. For her, it was a monumental decision of suppressing her personal values or upholding them. Parks held an unwavering belief in her right to be treated with dignity and equality, and, with a calm defiance that echoed much louder than any words, she responded to the bus driver's order with one word: "No". Rosa Parks' calm and firm 'no' rippled through history, shaping the contours of a nation's future. That single word, stemming from her deep-rooted personal values, lit a spark that quickly turned into a fire, marking the start of a 381-day boycott of the Montgomery bus system. Dr. Martin Luther King Jr. led The Montgomery Bus Boycott, and it was considered to be a massive act of civil disobedience. Thousands of Black citizens refused to use the city bus system, a direct hit to an industry that relied heavily on Black patrons. The ripple effect of Parks' decision and the subsequent boycott raised national and international awareness of the racial segregation prevalent in the southern United States and the fight against it. More than a year after Parks' decision to stay seated, the U.S. Supreme Court ruled segregation on public buses unconstitutional, a landmark victory for the civil rights movement. The Montgomery Bus Boycott marked the first large-scale demonstration against segregation and effectively launched the civil rights movement, leading to further campaigns and protests that eventually resulted in the Civil Rights Act of 1964.

Welcome to the reality that you make an impact, regardless of whether you are aware of it or even intend it. The mere act of your existence, of your breath moving in and out of your lungs, means you are creating ripples in the vast ocean of life. This mathematical theory is referred to as the Butterfly Effect. The Butterfly Effect theory suggests that the fluttering of a butterfly's wings could theoretically alter the trajectory of a tornado thousands of miles away. What it points to is how minor tweaks in initial conditions can snowball into dramatically different outcomes within complex systems. In essence, it emphasizes our universal interconnectivity and how the most seemingly random or insignificant of events can come to bear significant influence. This concept first took flight in the 1960s when Edward Lorenz, a mathematician and meteorologist, noticed a striking discrepancy while running weather prediction computer models. Inputting an initial condition of 0.506

instead of the full precision value of 0.506127 resulted in a vastly different weather scenario. This unexpected revelation illuminated the impossibility of long-term weather forecasting due to the hyper-sensitivity of initial conditions. The Butterfly Effect theory is now being considered a credible calculation method in many fields, including biology, economics, physics, and social science. In economics, for instance, minor fluctuations in consumer confidence can propel the economy into a boom or plunge it into a bust. Similarly, in ecology, a slight shift in a specific species' population can send an entire ecosystem's equilibrium into disarray.

Every single day, you are generating impacts, however subtle they may seem, on the world around you. Your actions, like ripples on the surface of a pond, extend far beyond your immediate sphere, influencing others in ways you might never consider or comprehend. Think of your habits as a consumer, for example. Each time you decide to purchase a product or service, you are casting a vote with your wallet, and tacitly endorsing the business practices of the company you are patronizing. Opting to buy from a company committed to ethical manufacturing means you are supporting not just the business but its inherent values. This ripple effect extends to the company's employees, the communities they operate within, and the environment at large. Using the same logic, analyze the impact of your resource usage. Every flick of a light switch, every turn of a tap, every decision about transportation, and every meal you eat – they all contribute to your environmental footprint. And so, when you make conscious choices, whether they are about conserving resources, choosing public transport, or opting for locally sourced food, you are wielding your influence for a more sustainable world, one decision at a time. Now, turn to your social interactions. Every conversation you engage in, every piece of advice you dole out, every smile you share – each one carries the potential to make someone's day a little bit brighter. Even the smallest acts of kindness ripples outwards and creates a positive cascade. For example, if you lend a helping hand to a colleague, they might feel inspired to pay it forward. This cycle of kindness cultivates a supportive and collaborative environment that bolsters productivity and enhances well-being, and it has all started with your decision to act kindly.

Your digital activities also have the same level of impact. The content you share and the comments you post on social media platforms steer opinions, disseminate information (or disinformation), and shape societal norms. Now, let us look at your personal growth decisions. When you invest in becoming a better version of yourself – acquiring new skills, surmounting harmful habits, fostering positivity – you are not only improving your life but setting an example for others and impacting their lives more positively. This ripple of inspiration, multiplied across individuals, contributes to a more enlightened society. To you, it may seem that your actions are just drops in an ocean, but these very drops make the ocean.

Hence, never underestimate the impact your decisions have on others' lives, nor undermine the influence you exert on your life and the world around you. Creating an impact is only bound by the limits of your creative thinking, and making a difference begins with making a decision of being selfless. Why don't you, considering your own identity and vision, make conscious decisions that contribute to bettering the world? Your decisions will have an impact on the world around you, regardless of your intentions. Why not be intentional about making everyone else's life easier and make your decisions in a way that has positive consequences for yourself and others? In the process, you will uncover a profound sense of joy and satisfaction that supersedes a self-centered lifestyle. Exercises 11.1 and 11.2 in the Appendix section will aid you in foreseeing -as much as humanly possible- the repercussions, consequences, and impact of your decision.

One more thing before we take off from here to the final pillar of the IVIC Decision-Making Framework©. Making a decision to volunteer is a powerful way to make this kind of impact. There are countless ways to support the less fortunate through voluntary service, and its popularity has soared as more people recognize that helping others is a potent means to nurture a sense of self-worth. Science corroborates this notion; research has shown that altruistic actions enhance overall wellness and infuse life with a newfound sense of purpose, something crucial for long-term happiness. If you are still hesitant about volunteering due to lack of time or energy, remember that each day that passes without you reaching out to help others is a missed opportunity. I encourage you to begin today by acknowledging the help you have received from others, and recognizing the chance you have to give back to a world that has gifted you so much. After all, we rise by lifting others.

Chapter 12

The Affordable Possibility

Now, to the final pillar of the IVIC Framework: calculating the trade-off of the choice you will make. Say you are at a crossroads with three diverging paths, each leading to a different destination - a forest, a beach, and a mountain. You have only one day to spend, and you can choose only one path. If you choose to explore the mountain, you lose the

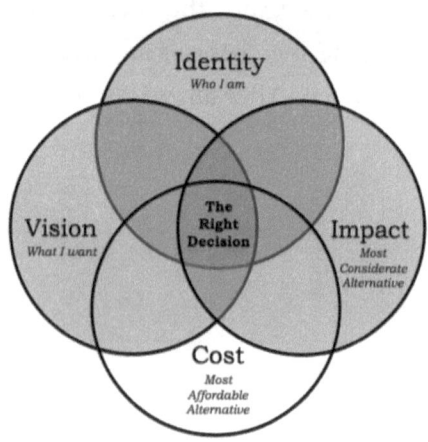

IVIC Decision-Making Framework©

experiences you could have had at the forest and the beach. Hence, in choosing the mountain, you lose the beach and the forest. This simply highlights that every choice has an inherent trade-off. Choosing, in its essence, is losing.

In the early 2000s, Netflix was a successful DVD rental business. Customers could rent DVDs online, and Netflix would send the DVDs to them through the mail. The model worked well and Netflix was quickly gaining popularity. Reed Hastings, one of Netflix's co-founders, could see the writing on the wall: The future was not in DVDs, it was in streaming services. He recognized the growth of the internet and realized that, in time, people would prefer to stream movies and TV shows directly to their devices rather than waiting for DVDs to arrive in the mail. So, Hastings made a decision to shift Netflix's focus from DVD rentals to streaming. In 2007, Netflix introduced its streaming service, allowing members to instantly watch television shows and movies on their personal computers. This was a risky decision; at the time, Netflix's DVD rental service was incredibly successful, and many people doubted whether customers would embrace streaming. Moreover, transitioning to a new business model was a complex, expensive process that required significant resources and time. The immediate effect of this decision was a drop in profits as the company invested heavily in the infrastructure and licensing agreements needed for streaming.

When Hastings chose to focus on streaming, he had to give up, or at least reduce, Netflix's focus on the flourishing DVD rental side of his business. On paper, this was a loss, and it was not entirely clear if the gamble would pay off. Many customers were unhappy with the change, Netflix's stock price fell, and the company faced significant backlash. However, Hastings was playing the long game. Fast forward to today, it is clear that his gamble paid off. Netflix has over 200 million subscribers worldwide and is one of the leading entertainment services globally at the time of writing this book.

Hastings had to let go of a successful business model to embrace an uncertain future. In the short term, this decision seemed like a loss. But in the long run, the choice to focus on streaming enabled Netflix to grow and succeed in ways that would not have been possible if it had remained a DVD rental service. The saying 'Choosing is losing' seems to capture the idea that when you make a choice, you are simultaneously letting go of other potential opportunities or paths - hence, in choosing, you *lose* those other possibilities. This concept is akin to what is known in economics as the *opportunity cost*. When you choose one thing, you lose the opportunity to do or have something else that you could have done or had with the same resources. This is a fundamental principle that people often use when making decisions. Ultimately, the point is to highlight the reality that your resources (time, energy, money, etc.) are limited, and you should be mindful of where and how you choose to use them. Making conscious and deliberate decisions while being aware of the potential trade-offs is an integral part of life. Simply, no one gets everything. I am sorry to bring this news to you if you had high hopes of getting literally everything you have ever wanted. The truth is, you will not find a person who is a 100% match of the spouse you had in your dreams. You will not have a *perfect* job that gives you everything while taking nothing from you in return. You will not live a *problem-free* life that is full of sunshine and roses. You must realize that having everything you want out of life is only a fairy tale, and that losing is what makes winning tasty! See, when you are making a decision, you are actually deciding what you are willing to let go of as much as what you want to take on. I believe this is when you sometimes face an inner conflict, and struggle to decide what you are prepared to lose more.

This sentiment resonates with a significant body of research in behavioral economics, psychology, and decision theory. Daniel Kahneman, a Nobel Prize-winning psychologist, along with Amos Tversky, extensively studied the concept of loss aversion and found that people feel the pain of loss about twice as much as they feel the joy of an equivalent gain. This principle, a cornerstone of their Prospect Theory, explains why people are often hesitant to make decisions that involve potential losses, even when the potential gain may be higher. The notion of choosing and losing also intersects with the paradox of choice, a concept popularized by psychologist Barry Schwartz. Schwartz argued that while some choice is undoubtedly better than none, more is not always better than less. In his research, Schwartz found that having many options to choose from can lead to feelings of anxiety, stress, dissatisfaction, and eventually indecisiveness. A study published in the

Journal of Personality and Social Psychology in 2000 reported that when participants were presented with 24 types of jam, they were less likely to make a purchase than those presented with only 6 types. On the neurological front, and according to research published in the journal Neuron, the difficulty in decision-making could also be traced back to the activity in two regions of the brain: the prefrontal cortex, associated with complex cognition like decision-making, and the striatum, associated with reward. The interaction between these two brain areas is what helps us weigh benefits against costs and make a decision. When the potential costs (or losses) appear to outweigh the benefits, decision-making can become a challenge, causing internal conflict.

One of my coaching clients, let us call her Jane, has been offered a high-paying job in a city far from her family and friends. Here, the problem Jane wanted to solve was not just deciding what she wanted, which was a new job with better career prospects and financial security. Jane came to me because she could not decide what she was prepared to give up – her proximity to loved ones and the comfort of a familiar environment. In this situation, Jane was faced with a tough decision – whatever she would decide to choose, she would have to lose something in return. Jane felt the inner conflict because her brain was weighing the rewards against the costs. She was excited about the new job (the reward), but the thought of leaving her family and friends behind was daunting (the cost). According to Kahneman and Tversky's Prospect Theory, the potential loss loomed larger in Jane's mind than the equivalent gain, making the decision particularly challenging. Making a decision often means accepting the loss of all the other attractive alternatives. This is a natural part of the decision-making process and an aspect of our lives that you might find challenging but is inevitable nonetheless. This all being said, I am about to make an argument that could turn out to be the most important reality of this whole reading experience, and I need you to know that I will be both straightforward and empathetic about it.

Listen, I do not mean to sound emotionless while talking about losses. If someone is hurting, their pain is real, regardless of how others perceive it. I know that because I -just like you and everyone else- have tasted it. I had to choose between people I love and my life's vision, secured jobs with big money and hustles I am passionate about, a fancy paycheck to be on TV and an opportunity to make a real impact on someone's life, act to please my friends and be authentic but lonely, stay warm at home with my family and go out in the cold to help somebody. It did hurt every time, because there was something to lose every time. Yet, as fundamental pain is in life, as powerful and transformative it can be.

The universe often presents its most arduous tests to those with remarkable resilience, and I now firmly believe that. I do not believe for a second that my significant tests began coincidentally when I became a trainer, coach, and writer. The combination of being a life coach and author grants me a powerful position and a significant responsibility. If I aspire to understand others' pain and suffering, I must experience it myself—and I have, profoundly. Feel free to dismiss this theory, but it resonates with me and has helped me come to terms with what many perceive as random events. From being rejected by society, to disconnecting from my family, to illness and accidents, to near-death experiences multiple times, to losing dear ones, trust me when I say I do know how real pain can be. Some of the pain came because of random, external, metaphysical reasons, some other pain came as a consequence of the uneducated decisions that I had made, and some other pain was inevitable as a consequence of educated ones. Either way, pain is real, and those who have the ability to comprehend this reality, and the courage to use it for their own advantage, are the ones who live the way they *truly* want.

Being aware of the cost of your decision is all about being fully aware of what you are letting go of, and being confident when making decisions is essentially being aware of what you want and what you *do not* want. With all the awareness you are taking away from this chapter, I would suggest you also check Exercise 12.1 in the Appendix section. Besides other tools you have used already, this one last piece in the IVIC Decision-Making Framework© will help you assess the cost of your decision.

Part 4 - The Execution Moment

"The oars of decision propel us forward; to look back
is to risk the drift into aimlessness."

Chapter 13

Executing Wisely

You have been through an extensive experience of self-awareness, unearthing what you want, and learning how to make significant decisions. You have all the reasons to have the clarity and confidence to make complex decisions. But let me bring your attention to something: making the right decision is something, and executing the decision properly is something different.

See, navigating the complex landscape of decision-making often requires an astute understanding that arriving at a decision is merely half the battle; it's the execution that truly tests your mettle. For instance, imagine a company that, after meticulous market analysis, discerns a golden opportunity to introduce a groundbreaking software tailored for young entrepreneurs. However, the launch becomes a case study in execution mishaps, from technical glitches to uninspiring marketing campaigns, culminating in missed targets and lackluster reviews. The brilliance of their initial decision was overshadowed by the shortcomings in its implementation. Visualize a firm that identifies a stellar candidate for a leadership role. Her credentials are impeccable, and her interview is inspiring. But once on board, due to lack of proper induction, clear communication about role expectations, or provision of necessary resources, she struggles to stay relevant to the organization's context, and the situation ends with both her and the organization missing out on the potential synergy.

On a more personal front, say you have always been passionate about environmental sciences and decide to start on a master's journey. The decision, rooted in passion and future prospects, is sound. But fast forward a few months, and instead of being engrossed in research and networking, you find yourself missing lectures, skimming through assignments, and being a passive participant in a course you were once thrilled about. The vision of enhancing your knowledge base, if not coupled with consistent effort and engagement, leads to unfulfilled potential. Switching gears to a dimension that resonates with almost everyone: health and fitness. The realization of leading a healthier life pushes you to enroll in the city's best gym. Yet, weeks into the membership, the initial enthusiasm wanes. Irregular workout schedules, coupled with unchecked diet habits, result in the scale barely budging. The commendable decision to prioritize health meets the harsh reality of inconsistent follow-through.

The key question we are answering in this chapter is: Now that you have clarity on what you want to do and have made a confident decision, *how* are you going to stay confident and resilient in the face of potential challenges? To do so, we first need to define what wisdom is. From my perspective, wisdom is what is *suitable*. To dress wisely is to make your appearance suitable to the place you are in. To speak wisely is to say the suitable things, the suitable way, to the suitable people, in the suitable time. To behave wisely is to do the suitable things, in the suitable way, in the suitable time. And so, to craft a detailed action plan and make sure you are wisely executing on your decision, you need to have a full understanding of what you would consider to be *suitable* in a given context. Having a plan and a backup plan to the plan is a must, but not enough. Being prepared for challenges means cultivating a mindset that can adapt to the unexpected context, and confidence is something you build through knowledge, understanding, and trust in yourself and those around you, not only by having a plan.

As solid as your plan might be, you can never expect what challenges and roadblocks will arise along the way - you can predict the context, and therefore you cannot really define what is suitable until you arrive at the context. But confidence is to realize that you have the power to navigate this context with wisdom, resilience, and grace. In your hands lies the potential to turn your decision into a reality, not merely through action but through understanding, empathy, and an unshakeable belief in what you can achieve. This is how you ensure that the way you execute your decision is wise. And so, what we will do in this chapter is to make sure that you have both the plan to execute the decision and the right mindset to do it in a suitable manner.

Based on my own journey, I can attest that things seldom go according to plan. Life's inherent unpredictability makes it nearly impossible to adhere to a rigid plan. Yet, a clear plan on how you will execute your decision serves as a benchmark and a guide in making relevant decisions. The fact that you already have a plan instills confidence in your steps as you stride toward your goal, because you have a direction already. Imagine crossing a busy one-way street with no pedestrian crossings, the movement of cars is unpredictable, and you need to dodge them swiftly. You can only do this if you have a clear view of your destination, namely the other side of the road, right? Now, imagine the same situation but with a blindfold on your eyes. Quite daunting, isn't it? See, making a decision is a good start, but you must have a clear idea *how* you will execute this decision.

Personally, I have changed life courses three times and career paths five times, all in less than fifteen years. We are talking about a new life purpose every 5 years, and a new career direction every 3 years. Before you judge me, I am mentioning this now for a good reason: I want to help you distinguish between changing directions and not having a direction at all. It is analogous to the difference between updating your mobile phone's software and not having any software installed in the first place. Adjusting the ship's course toward a new destination is not the same as navigating without a compass. One scenario suggests an active stance, while the other implies passivity. A study by psychologists Patrick Hill and Nicholas Turiano discovered that individuals with a clear sense of purpose had a lower risk of developing disabilities and had increased longevity over a decade. Their research implies that having a life direction boosts psychological well-being and has concrete physical health benefits. Other psychological research has shown that setting specific goals and devising a plan to attain them significantly boosts motivation and the likelihood of success. Psychologists Edwin Locke and Gary Latham found that individuals who set clear, challenging goals outperformed those with vague or no goals. Therefore, having a life direction, even if it morphs over time, provides a sense of purpose. Yes, the objectives may evolve, and the strategies may shift, but there is always a guiding force propelling you forward. The path you tread may twist and turn, and lead to unforeseen places, and this is completely fine as long as a clear path always exists.

Take Jeff Bezos, the founder of Amazon, for instance. He started his career on Wall Street, then pivoted when he recognized the untapped potential of the internet and decided to establish Amazon. This change of direction, fueled by a vision and a purpose, paved the way for his monumental success. Contrast this with a directionless life, akin to a ship drifting in the ocean, without a compass or a destination. If you believe that because things never go according to plan then there is no point of having a plan at all, you will find yourself in a reactive state every time you have to make a decision, and you will have no choice but to surrender control to external circumstances rather than proactively shape your own destiny. Life decisions are like crossing a busy one-way street with no pedestrian crossings. It is hard to predict the flow of traffic, and there is not a straight line to guide you safely across. But if you know your destination, you can move confidently, adjusting your path as needed to avoid obstacles. Now, imagine trying to cross the street blindfolded. Without a clear vision of where you are going, the mere task of crossing the street becomes immensely more challenging. You will not be able to see the obstacles in your path, and each step you take will become more uncertain and potentially dangerous.

The point being: Changing directions is not a sign of aimlessness. Rather, it is a reflection of self-awareness, and being wise enough to change the plan, and adapt to the context when your current path no longer serves your purpose or values. Yes, it does take courage and a growth mindset to pivot toward a direction that resonates more deeply with the evolving context of life situations. Actually, I find changing directions to be an opportunity for self-improvement and personal transformation. The world around us is constantly evolving, and staying relevant requires being open to change and adjusting course accordingly. A sense of direction gives you purpose, even if the path changes. The goals may evolve, and the strategies may shift, but the guiding principle remains. The journey, the So, ask yourself, are you driving your life, or are you being driven by it? Exercise 13.1 in the Appendix section is designed to help you introspect a life direction.

I told you the story about me meeting with the Buddhist monks in Nepal and shared with you what they taught me about confidence, and you and I had a good discussion about how having a purpose automatically boosts confidence. While being confident in your skin is an automatic byproduct of self-awareness, being confident in your plan, however, is another story. You can be confident in who you are and how capable you are in facing the challenges on the way. Yet, having confidence in your own plan is the first step to achieving that robust state of mind. Let me share with you a few lessons that Eliza Hamilton taught me.

Born into a prestigious family, Eliza Hamilton was no stranger to society's upper echelons. But she had never expected to face the trials that would befall her after the death of her husband, Alexander Hamilton, a prominent figure in the American Revolution. Her world, once stable and secure, crumbled in an instant, leaving her a widow with many young children, in a period when women had few rights or opportunities. Without faltering, she embarked on a mission to honor her husband's legacy. She had no roadmap to follow; she relied only on her skills, knowledge, and an unwavering belief in her mission. Her most significant project was compiling Alexander's extensive writings for publication. This task was not for the faint-hearted, though; Alexander had left behind thousands of pages of letters, reports, essays, and notes, each carrying a part of America's history and his personal thoughts and ideas. Eliza's project required meticulous planning and organization. She would have to decipher her late husband's sometimes chaotic thoughts, arrange them in an understandable order, and present them to the world. This endeavor took over fifty years of her life. It was a massive task that required patience, attention to detail, and an undying commitment to her mission.

Throughout the years, Eliza demonstrated resourcefulness, and sought the help of historians, family members, and anyone who had known or worked with Alexander. She was not shy to tap into her network, knowing that each interaction would bring her one step closer to realizing her goal. Her journey was not smooth sailing, of course; there were countless roadblocks along the way. Yet, Eliza adapted, continuously reassessing her strategies and adjusting her course of action. She understood that even the best-laid plans could encounter unforeseen obstacles. When difficulties arose, she was ready with contingency plans, never letting setbacks stop her progress.

If we look closely into Eliza's story, we can extract five key lessons on how to set a proper, robust, and holistic plan. Upcoming are the five key lessons with application exercises for you to critically analyze your plan, and make adjustments as needed. By the end of this chapter, you will have a comprehensive, feasible plan with contingencies for potential risks.

Lesson 1: Be a goal-oriented pragmatist

Having a vision for your future is a must if you want to have a clear direction for your life, and keep your spirits and motivation up. However, having a vision without a clear action plan becomes more of daydreaming than reality. Start your action plan by outlining the specific goal you want to achieve. A specific goal is the clearly defined target that you will aim for. If you are looking to start a business, this could mean defining your target market, the nature of your product or service, and what success looks like in terms of sales or growth. If your goal is losing weight, the objective might be losing a particular number of pounds within a specific timeframe. After you have set a goal, you break these goals into smaller tasks, and every large goal can be broken down into smaller, more manageable pieces. For example, if your objective is to write a novel, the smaller tasks could include outlining the plot, developing characters, writing individual chapters, and revising the manuscript. If you are planning a family vacation, the tasks might include selecting a destination, booking flights, reserving accommodations, and planning activities.

Deadlines are vital to keeping your plan on track. If you are launching a new product, you might set deadlines for product development, marketing, production, and distribution. If your goal is to save money for a down payment on a house, you might establish monthly savings targets leading up to the date you want to purchase. Deadlines engender a sense of urgency and help you avoid procrastination. Moreover, identifying the resources needed is crucial for any plan. If you are aiming to start a community garden, the resources might include volunteers, gardening tools, seeds, and a plot of land. If you are working toward a career promotion, you may need to invest time in additional training, find a mentor, or network with influential people in your field. Finally, monitoring how your plan is progressing is the continuous process of checking your progress and adjusting the plan as needed. Suppose you are training for a marathon and suffer an injury; you may need to alter your training schedule and seek physical therapy. If you are building a startup and a competitor enters the market, you may need to revise your marketing strategy. This is when you might need to be flexible because unexpected challenges and opportunities will inevitably arise. So, my dear friend, let us make sure you have a plan in place! Exercise 13.2 in the Appendix section is all about setting an inclusive plan.

Lesson 2: Avoid confirmation bias

The Titanic was touted as the "unsinkable" ship. This tag, complemented by the luxurious fittings and advanced technology for its time, created an aura of invincibility around the Titanic. Even after warnings of icebergs in the ship's path, the Titanic continued at full speed. The fervent belief that the ship was unsinkable was so strong that it biased the decisions of its captain and crew, leading them to disregard critical information that contradicted their belief. The ship's radio operators received six messages from other ships warning of ice, but these messages were not taken seriously. This was because the radio operators were more focused on sending passenger messages and because they, along with the rest of the crew, were influenced by the prevailing belief in the ship's invincibility. Even when the ship eventually hit an iceberg, the officers did not fully grasp the extent of the damage. Passengers were casually informed of the situation without emphasizing the seriousness, and therefore, the evacuation procedures started too late.

The confirmation bias - the firm belief in the ship's unsinkability - led to the downplaying and ignoring of contradicting information and, ultimately, to one of the biggest maritime disasters in history. Wouldn't you agree it is best that you make sure your Titanic will sail confidently and safely? Exercise 13.3 in the Appendix section will help you conduct a feasibility audit for your plan, and do a reality check on what is truly possible, and what is not.

Lesson 3: Plan B is as important as Plan A

Apollo 13 was the third mission intended to land on the moon. The crew launched from Kennedy Space Center, Florida, on April 11, 1970. However, the lunar landing was aborted after an oxygen tank in the service module failed two days into the mission. The phrase "Houston, we've had a problem," reported by astronaut Jack Swigert, has since become a part of popular culture, signifying an unforeseen problem. While NASA had run extensive simulations and developed various contingency plans, this was the first time anyone had anticipated this specific scenario. However, the meticulous culture of risk assessment and planning for potential problems enabled NASA's mission control and the astronauts to quickly adapt to the crisis. The mission quickly changed from a moon landing to simply returning the astronauts safely to Earth. The crew had to execute a critical engine burn to adjust their trajectory, using the moon's gravity to slingshot them back toward Earth. This was an extremely risky maneuver, but it was successfully performed. Back on Earth, teams of engineers scrambled to work out solutions for other problems caused by the explosion, such as scrubbing the build-up of carbon dioxide from the air in the spacecraft and conserving both water and power for the duration of the journey home.

Despite the life-threatening situation, the crew returned safely to Earth on April 17 due to the well-executed contingency plans and the ability to assess and respond to risks in real time. The Apollo 13 mission is now often called a "successful failure" because of the experience gained in rescuing the crew and the key lessons learned about spacecraft design and contingency planning. Let us make sure that if your plan fails, it fails successfully. Exercise 13.4 in the Appendix section will help you conduct a quick risk assessment and set a plan B.

Lesson 4: Learn from previous performance

Serena Williams is one of the most dominant and successful tennis players in the history of the sport. Her father, Richard Williams, instilled in her and her sister Venus a love for the game and the drive to excel from a very young age. Her natural talent was undeniable, and what set her apart was her ability to reflect on her performances, both good and bad. After a match, win or lose, Serena would watch recordings of her play. She would study not only her own game but her opponents' as well. She was keen to reflect on what she did right and what she needed to improve. Serena's reflection on past successes and failures has been a vital part of her training regimen, allowing her to make the necessary adjustments to her game and helping her to adapt to new opponents and play styles.

An example of this reflective practice in action came after her surprising loss at the 2012 French Open's first round. Rather than being discouraged, Serena used this setback as a learning experience. She reflected on what went wrong and sought the help of a new coach, Patrick Mouratoglou. Together, they analyzed her performance, recognizing the successes within her game that needed to be highlighted and the areas that required improvement. She came back to win the French Open the following year. This victory was a turning point in her career, and her reflective practice played a vital role. Exercise 13.5 in the Appendix section is a good reflection tool, and will help you reflect and analyze your previous performance.

Lesson 5: You are who you think you are

Before he became famous as an actor, Silvester Stallone -also known in Hollywood as Sly- was going through a very tough time. He had no money, his wife was pregnant, and he was living in a small apartment in New York City. Sly had a dream to be an actor, but faced constant rejection and was repeatedly turned down at auditions due to his slurred speech and unconventional looks. But Sly never stopped believing in himself, and consistently practiced positive self-talk, telling himself that he had what it took to succeed in the industry. One day, he watched a boxing match between Muhammad Ali and Chuck Wepner, which inspired him to write the script for "Rocky." Sly finished the script in three days, and when he presented it to the producers, they loved it. However, they did not want him to act in it – they wanted a well-known star. But Sly was persistent and insisted that he would only sell the script if he could play the lead role. Despite facing immense financial difficulties, he held onto his script until he found producers who agreed to let him play the lead role. Rocky ended up winning three Oscars and turned Stallone into a star overnight. The power of positive self-talk is clear, and I am curious: What do you keep telling yourself? Exercise 13.6 is about bringing your self-belief back.

Setting Boundaries

I believe the only remaining point left unaddressed, to answer the question "How can I successfully execute my decision?", is setting personal boundaries. You may already know that personal boundaries are like invisible lines you draw around yourself to protect your energy, your well-being, and your integrity. These are the limits you set with yourself and others to define what you find acceptable and unacceptable in your relationships, your work, and your personal life. But how can you set these boundaries, especially in a world filled with conflicting expectations, societal pressures, and the relentless demands of modern life? Here's how.

The first step is to keep an eye on your Authenticity Pyramid©. Never forget what you believe deep inside, what motivates you, what you value the most, what you are most passionate about, and that you have the ability to set a mission for your own life. Just as you would not build a house without a solid foundation, setting boundaries requires a deep awareness of who you are and what you want. Reflect on the experiences that have shaped you, your dreams, and what you want your life to look like. Define what makes you feel uncomfortable or drained and what invigorates you and brings joy. This self-awareness is your compass in setting boundaries that truly resonate with who you are.

The Authenticity Pyramid©

Next, you must clearly communicate these boundaries. It is one thing to know what your boundaries are, but quite another to articulate them to others. You cannot expect others to respect your boundaries if they do not know what they are. Speaking up might feel uncomfortable initially, but expressing your needs does not make you selfish or inflexible, it makes you self-worthy. When you clearly express your boundaries to others, you end up protecting yourself and consequently enhancing your overall well-being. For a pro tip, you do not have to be aggressive or defensive while doing it. Always be empathetic, because your goal is to communicate what makes you feel comfortable, not to make the other person feel uncomfortable. At the end of the day, you would not want to set your own boundaries to relieve yourself from the pressure by hurting someone else, would you?

Setting boundaries requires consistency and reinforcement. You may find that others test or push against these boundaries, especially if the boundaries you have set conflict with what they expect from you. You might find it incredibly challenging when these people are close to you, like friends or family. I encourage you to stay true to what you have established, and acknowledge that enforcing boundaries may be an uncomfortable but necessary step in respecting your own worth.

You do not need to lock yourself into a set of unchangeable rules; these are more of prison bars than boundaries. Setting boundaries is a dynamic and evolving journey that aligns with your growth and changing circumstances. Reflect, reassess, and adjust as needed while always keeping in mind that these boundaries are the enablers that allow you to make decisions that lead to a life that is authentically yours. In your path to setting personal boundaries, you empower yourself to make wise decisions without giving up to societal pressure. Yes, this requires courage, clarity, and consistency. If you are wondering how to go about applying all of this, Exercise 13.7 in the Appendix section is an excellent tool for you.

Chapter 14

Post-Decision Thoughts

In the late 1950s, Miles Davis was at the pinnacle of his career in jazz, pioneering a whole new sound with his album "Kind of Blue." But as the 1960s unfolded, he felt an itch for something new. The world of music was changing; rock and funk were rising, and jazz was viewed by some as a thing of the past. Miles began to wonder, "What if I am left behind?" That doubt turned into a decision: he decided to change his music. It was not a smooth transition; many of his fans were dismayed by his new direction, and critics were harsh. The album "Bitches Brew," released in 1969, was a radical departure from his earlier works. It blended jazz with rock to create something entirely new. Some loved it, but others were disappointed, and the doubt crept back in. Did he make the right decision? What if he had stayed the course? Instead of succumbing to doubt, Miles pressed on. He said once in an interview, "I have to change. It is like a curse". That relentless pursuit of growth, even in the face of doubt, made him a musical icon who transcended genres.

Doubt can be a nagging companion, especially after you have taken a significant step in a direction you once felt sure about. I am talking about this irritating voice, whispering "What if?", and painting images of alternate realities. "What if I had chosen differently?" "What would have happened if I had taken that other path?" You have made a decision, and perhaps you did not achieve what you wanted, or were met with unexpected challenges. Doubt begins to creep in, testing your resolve and shaking your confidence. This is a universal experience that knows no borders, age, or culture. It is natural for us, humans, to question, wonder, and even regret. We have all been there at some point in our lives, and that is why I have confidence that this chapter will speak to you, wherever you are in life.

Where is this doubt coming from, though? Well, many reasons. Internally, your past experiences shape your present doubts. That time when you were a teenager and chose to join a sports team only to face criticism from friends, or, professionally, when you proposed a project at work that did not pan out, are memories that cause you to question your current decisions, like choosing a new hobby or launching a business venture. This explains how self-confidence plays a role. You might have felt unsure while selecting an outfit for a special occasion because you fear judgments about your appearance, or when accepting a leadership role in a big project. Also, the complexity of the decision itself can sow doubt. Choosing a college major might be as perplexing as deciding on a new market strategy for your business. The more factors involved, the more room for doubt.

Externally, opinions of others affect you. Your family might question your choice of a life partner, just as your colleagues at work might challenge your decision to implement a new workflow process. Both personal and professional spheres are filled with voices that might not align with your choices. Societal norms and expectations can pressure you. Perhaps you have decided to take a non-traditional career path, like becoming an artist, and now have to face societal skepticism, or choosing to remain single in a culture that values marriage. These decisions might stir doubt due to societal expectations. The media's influence is pervasive as well. A trending article about the benefits of a vegetarian diet might make you question your diet decisions. Similarly, a report on the booming tech industry might cause you to second-guess your choice to invest in traditional manufacturing. But, most of all, life's inherent unpredictability adds to the doubt. A sudden rainstorm might have you doubting your decision to camp for the weekend, just as unexpected market changes might make you question your business expansion plans.

How to deal with all of this, I hear you ask? Well, embracing doubt is your first step. Doubt is a natural reaction to uncertainty, whether you are a teenager deciding to pursue music or a senior executive contemplating a business merger. When you acknowledge the uncertainty, you transform it from a barrier into a guidepost. Next, reflect on what matters most to you. Aligning decisions with core values and long-term objectives offers clarity. This alignment resonates whether you are a young couple pondering buying their first home or a community leader planning a social project. Your values are the compass that will steer you through the uncertainty, and incremental goals ease the decision-making process. If you are relocating from Buenos Aires to Berlin or introducing a new product in Tokyo, breaking it down into manageable steps breeds confidence and makes progress feel achievable. Perfection is not the goal; growth is. Accept that not all the decisions you make will be perfect, and focus on learning from your mistakes to keep moving forward.

Mindfulness is a practice that alleviates doubt and anxiety. Being present in the moment with your choices is a game changer; whether you are a retiree picking up a new hobby or a tech startup management team making hiring decisions. Revisiting and reflecting on your decisions without endless rumination is a delicate balance, and it is healthy to look back periodically and make new decisions as needed. At all costs, avoid getting stuck in a loop of guilt or regret.

Lastly, celebrate, please. Celebrate the courage it takes to make these decisions. Every choice you make contributes to your unique journey. Your decisions, with all their complexity, uncertainty, and potential pains and gains, are a tapestry that only you can weave. Your life is a winding road, filled with intersections of doubt and alleys of anxiety. It is also a path of wisdom, growth, and potential. I have enclosed Exercise 14.1 in the Appendix section if you wish to go about this step by step. Afterwards, come back to the beginning of the process. It seems, my friend, that if you are wondering whether you have made the right decision or not, you have a new decision to make!

Managing a wrong decision

In the early 20th century, René Blondlot, a French physicist, claimed to have discovered a new element called "N-rays." His discovery was celebrated and accepted until a young American physicist, Robert Wood, revealed that it was an observational error. Rather than defending his mistake or letting it ruin his career, Blondlot chose to learn from it. He accepted that he had been wrong and continued to contribute valuable physics research. His decision to correct his mistake and move on had a profound impact on both his life and the scientific community. Admitting a mistake took courage, and his professional life did not end with this mistake; it merely shifted direction. His willingness to acknowledge and learn from his mistakes allowed him to grow as a researcher. The N-ray debacle led to more rigorous standards for observation and reporting in the scientific community, and Blondlot's ability to correct his mistakes played a part in fostering a culture of integrity and diligence. Mistakes in his professional life affected his personal reputation and self-image, but Blondlot preserved his professional standing and personal dignity by handling his errors with grace and humility.

When you face the mistakes, you make with honesty and resilience, you transform them into stepping stones toward greater success. Learning from mistakes and moving forward is a mindset that requires both courage and introspection. I understand that acknowledging mistakes might not be easy for some, but doing so leads to profound growth and experience. Error Management Theory teaches us that making and reflecting on mistakes is a powerful learning tool that enhances future performance. This is how you can systematically review what went wrong and develop strategies to avoid similar mistakes in the future. It is the same in your personal life by the way. Perhaps you have faced a failed relationship. It is painful and often shrouded in regret and guilt, but there are mistakes analysis and forward planning exercises that can guide you to understand what went wrong and how to move forward. Asking probing questions, reflecting on your actions and emotions, and consciously planning your future steps can lead to healing and growth. Exercise 14.2 in the Appendix section will help you reflect and correct a wrong decision.

Closing Remarks

No one can deny that our control as humans on the course of life is limited. Yet, whether you believe you live one life or multiple, you own today and everything that happens in it. The stimulus may be internal in the form of an idea you have, or external in the form of a situation you find yourself in. Either way, the decision of how you respond to these stimuli is yours. You, and only you, are responsible for the decisions you make. In navigating the complexities of decision-making, a process so intrinsic to the human experience, you have encountered both the subtleties and the grandeur of choice. The journey you have undertaken within these pages has been one to enhance your mastery over decisions, and turn seemingly ordinary moments into profound inflection points that shape your destiny.

The essence of every transformative journey is, undeniably, self-awareness. As you have gleaned from the preceding chapters, this quality is a necessity. Truly understanding yourself means delving deep into your beliefs, values, and aspirations. When faced with life's relentless array of choices, having this profound understanding is akin to possessing a compass, ensuring you never lose your way. Whether in personal realms or the tumultuous world of business, a sharp and intimate self-awareness becomes the foundation upon which your decisions are made, both with clarity and confidence. Of course, this clarity is not attained overnight; it demands the courage to confront past errors and the wisdom to see them not as successes and failures, but as lessons. Every mistake or oversight is a growth opportunity—a chance to refine your approach and sharpen your decision-making prowess. The art of learning from errors is rooted in actionable introspection, and mining insights from past experiences to ensure the path ahead is illuminated by the wisdom of hindsight.

Professionally, every leadership role and entrepreneurial venture thrives based on the quality of decisions made. From conceptualizing business strategies to nurturing team dynamics, decisions dictate trajectories. The invaluable tools and techniques you have been acquainted with aim to empower your professional choices, ensuring your vision is both clear and impactful. Similarly, in the personal spheres of your life, the decisions you make shape your narrative. Here, your choices morph into memories, aspirations turn into achievements, and hopes become realities. As if you are having a dance of decisions, where every move is choreographed by the choices you make. While the outcomes of these choices are undeniably significant, there is an inherent beauty in the journey of decision-making itself. It is a path punctuated by introspection, challenges, revelations, and growth—a path that is as rewarding as the milestones it leads to.

In the backdrop of all this is the importance of moving forward. Decisions, by their very nature, propel motion. And while you are equipped with tools, techniques, and insights, it is imperative to harness the energy of momentum. Stagnation is the antithesis of growth, and thus, as you close this chapter, know that it is merely the beginning of countless more. The wisdom of the pages empowers you to stand at the threshold of endless opportunities, each beckoning you to shape them with your touch. Each decision becomes a testament to your journey, a reflection of your growth, and an emblem of your unique narrative. Life, in its vast expanse, offers a canvas, and your decisions—the brushstrokes—craft a masterpiece that is uniquely yours. When you stand at a potential decision with a brush in hand, paint with passion, intent, and the drive to make your story a worth-telling one.

As you turn the last pages of this book, fortified with newfound insights and perspectives, I invite you to cherish the empowerment that comes with conscious decision-making. Embrace the uncertainties, for they are but opportunities in disguise. Relish the challenges, for they sculpt your resilience. And, above all, celebrate your journey of choices, for it is the essence of life itself. Your path is illuminated, your compass set, and a world of decisions awaits. Make them count, shape your narrative, and craft a life story that resonates with purpose, passion, and unparalleled authenticity.

About The Author

M.E. Wasfi is a professional leadership & executive coach, a keynote speaker, and a business consultant based in Dubai, UAE. Wasfi promotes the values of freedom, responsibility, empathy, and respect. His professional vision is using science and logic to liberate individual potential; through coaching, training, and writing. Besides running a successful coaching business, Wasfi's consulting work spans various sectors including government institutes, startups, and corporations to develop and lead leadership development programs tailored to various industry needs. His current professional commitments include his role as Founder and CEO of IVIC Decisions FZCO, the global leadership development organization based in Dubai, UAE, and the City Lead-Dubai for Global Class. His professional experience extends to Edtech, Talent Management, Business Strategy, and more.

Wasfi began his professional journey in the startup ecosystem, spending the initial years of his professional career in that arena. Between 2012 and 2017, his focus shifted to humanitarian work. He collaborated with NGOs and operated in over 15 countries across Asia and Africa, aiming to alleviate the challenges posed by terrorism in these regions. Returning to the corporate domain, Wasfi channeled his diverse experiences to aid business leaders in their growth trajectories. Since his return to the business world, he has coached over 2,000 leaders of more than 100 different nationalities and in more than 25 different markets. His insights into business consultancy, leadership development, and executive coaching have also led to speaking engagements at events such as the Edtech World Forum London and Centuro Global Expansion conferences. You can know more about Wasfi and get in touch with him by visiting www.ivicdecisions.com.

Appendix

Exercise 1.1: How conscious are you?

<u>Step 1</u>: Set aside a specific time each day, preferably for at least 10-15 minutes, when you can engage in this exercise without distractions. Find a quiet and comfortable space where you can sit or lie down.

<u>Step 2</u>: Start by bringing your attention to your body. Close your eyes and take a few deep breaths, allowing yourself to relax. With your eyes still closed, slowly scan your body from head to toe, noticing any sensations, tensions, or areas of comfort. Pay attention to the physical sensations without judgment or the need to change anything.

<u>Step 3</u>: Gradually expand your awareness to your immediate environment. Begin to notice the sounds around you—the hum of appliances, birds chirping, distant traffic, or any other sounds.

<u>Step 4</u>: Pay attention to the sensations on your skin—the temperature, the feeling of clothing against your body, or any other tactile sensations. Then, focus on any scents in the air—the aroma of food, fresh air, or any other smells.

<u>Step 5</u>: If you feel comfortable, open your eyes and observe the visuals—the colors, shapes, and objects in your surroundings.

<u>Step 6</u>: Now shift your attention inward and observe your thoughts and emotions without getting caught up in them. Notice the patterns of your thoughts, the content of your mind, and the emotions that arise. Allow them to come and go without trying to control or suppress them. Just observe them with curiosity and non-judgment.

<u>Step 7</u>: Bring your attention back to your breath—the sensation of the breath entering and leaving your body. Stay with this awareness of your breath, grounding yourself in the present moment. Whenever your mind wanders, gently guide your attention back to your breath.

<u>Step 8:</u> Take a few moments to reflect on your experience. Ask yourself the following questions:

- How present and conscious was I during the exercise?
- Did I notice any moments of distraction or wandering thoughts?
- How often did I bring myself back to the present moment?
- How did it feel to observe my thoughts and emotions without getting caught up in them?
- How can I bring this level of consciousness and presence into my daily life?

Exercise 1.2: Discovering Your Dynamic Self

<u>Step 1:</u> Write down the labels or definitions that you feel are currently defining you. Ask yourself, "What labels have I consciously or unconsciously adopted, and how do they influence my behavior and choices?"

<u>Step 2:</u> For each label, ask yourself: "Is this really true? Does it encompass all that I am?" Reflect on instances that contradict these labels. Ask yourself, "How have I behaved in ways that contradict this label? What experiences challenge this definition?"

<u>Step 3:</u> Consider your multifaceted nature. Write down these diverse aspects of yourself. Ask yourself, "How am I more complex than these labels? What are the different roles and characteristics that make up who I am?"

<u>Step 4:</u> Recognize the shared human experiences behind these complexities. Write down universal roles you fill. Ask yourself, "What connects me to others? How do these universal roles help me understand myself in relation to the world?"

<u>Step 5:</u> Imagine a version of yourself free from the constraints of rigid labels. Ask yourself, "What would I do, think, or feel if I were free from these labels? How would this liberate my approach to life?"

<u>Step 6:</u> Outline specific actions or attitudes that align with your new understanding of yourself. Ask yourself, "What practical steps can I take to embody this liberated self? How will I know when I am aligning with this vision?"

<u>Step 7:</u> Regularly reflect on your progress. Adjust as needed. Ask yourself, "How am I progressing towards my intentions? What adjustments might help me grow further?"

<u>Step 8:</u> If you find this process particularly challenging, consider seeking professional support. I am always available to help!

Exercise 2.1: Are you being dramatic?

This exercise will help you reflect on different areas of your life, and observe if your mind is holding you back from focusing on what matters and acting responsibly.

<u>Step 1:</u> Find a quiet and comfortable space where you can reflect without distractions. Take a few deep breaths to center yourself and bring your attention to the present moment.

<u>Step 2:</u> Spot 3 key areas in your life to reflect on your roles in. For example, you could focus on being the employee or leader at work, a parent or a sibling at home, and team player in the sports team.

<u>Step 3:</u> For each of the 3 key areas you chose to focus on, think of one recent problem you faced. It could be an undesirable position or a complex situation that needed your attention.

<u>Step 4:</u> Reflect on your thoughts, emotions, and behaviors related to each of the situations. Ask yourself the following questions:

- Am I exaggerating the situation or blowing things out of proportion?
- Do I tend to react emotionally without considering alternative perspectives?
- Am I seeking attention or validation through my dramatic behavior?
- Are my reactions causing unnecessary conflict or stress?
- Do I take responsibility for my actions, or do I blame others for the outcomes?
- Which of the three dramatic roles (victim, rescuer, prosecutor) do I tend to play more often? (*hint: if the answer is any of the three, or all of the three roles, you are pretty normal!*)

<u>Step 5:</u> Explore the underlying reasons for your dramatic behavior. Consider past experiences, insecurities, fears, or unmet needs that may be influencing your reactions. Why are you reacting this way?

Exercise 2.2: Adapting a growth mindset

<u>Step 1:</u> Start by understanding what a growth mindset is.
- What do you think a growth mindset is?
- Can you identify a person who embodies this mindset? What behaviors do they exhibit?

<u>Step 2:</u> Identify your current mindset
- When facing a new challenge, what thoughts and feelings arise?
- Can you recall a time when you gave up on something? What held you back?

<u>Step 3:</u> Address your fears and perspective to failure.
- What does failure mean to you?
- Can you share a story when fear of failure stopped you from trying something new?
- How might viewing failure as a learning opportunity change your approach to new challenges?

<u>Step 4:</u> Visualize stepping out of your comfort zone
- What activities or situations make you feel most comfortable? Why?
- What might you learn or gain by stepping outside of these comfort zones?
- Can you commit to trying something that feels uncomfortable this week?

<u>Step 5:</u> Utilize constructive feedback.
- Have you ever received feedback that helped you grow? What was it, and how did it feel?
- How can you seek out feedback regularly to help you improve?

<u>Step 6:</u> Redefine what success is to you.
- How do you currently define success?
- How could focusing on growth and learning, instead of only the end result, enrich your life?

Step 7: Embrace a mindset of responsibility and proactivity.

- Can you identify a situation where taking responsibility led to personal growth?
- How can being proactive, rather than reactive, change your outcomes?

Step 8: Create your own growth mindset manifesto.

- Based on what you've explored, what does a growth mindset mean to you now?
- What specific steps will you take to cultivate this mindset in your daily life?

Exercise 3.1: The Five-Step Decisional Balance Sheet

This exercise is built on the principle of cognitive behavioral therapy, a technique often employed to manage anxiety disorders. However, you don't have to have a disorder to benefit from it. Think of it as a practical tool for your emotional toolkit.

Step 1: First things first, jot down the decision you're grappling with. Try to frame it as a choice, not a looming, daunting inevitability. For instance, "Should I accept the job offer in another city?" is a healthier frame than "I have to decide if I'm uprooting my life."

Step 2: Now, make a list of all the pros and cons associated with the decision. Be honest with yourself. For the pros, consider both immediate and long-term benefits. For the cons, think about the potential negative outcomes and their impact. (*refer to The Clarity Moment and The Decision Moment sections for relevant frameworks*)

Step 3: Beside each pro and con, write down the emotion it evokes. It could be excitement, fear, hope, stress, anything, just to acknowledge them.

Step 4: Now, rate your current level of anxiety about the decision on a scale of 1 to 10. Jot it down.

Step 5: Take a break for a day or two. Let your mind process all you've jotted down. Then, revisit your list. Notice any shifts in your feelings? Has your anxiety level changed? What's influencing this change?

Exercise 3.2: The Fear Map

This approach borrows concepts from mindfulness and cognitive behavioral therapy, and it's aimed at helping you understand your fear, not conquer it. After all, understanding is the first step towards management.

<u>Step 1:</u> Start by clearly defining your fear related to the decision you're about to make. Write it down in a single sentence. Specificity is key. So, instead of saying "I'm afraid of making the wrong choice", try something like "I'm afraid of taking the new job and failing."

<u>Step 2:</u> Close your eyes and imagine the scenario that scares you. Let the scene play out in your mind. Yes, it's uncomfortable, but it's also important.

<u>Step 3:</u> Now, identify what emotions this visualization stirs up. Is it anxiety, shame, regret, disappointment? Write these down next to your fear statement. There's power in naming what you're feeling.

<u>Step 4:</u> Are there negative thoughts that accompany these emotions? Write those down too. They might be things like "I'm not good enough" or "I always mess up."

<u>Step 5:</u> For every negative thought you've listed, write down a counter-statement that challenges this negativity. For instance, "I always mess up" could be countered with "I've succeeded in new roles before, and I can do it again."

<u>Step 6:</u> Now, with your counter-statements in mind, reassess the fear you initially defined. Has it changed in intensity or nature? Write down this reflection.

<u>Step 7:</u> Finally, consider what actions could help mitigate your fear. Could it be seeking advice, acquiring more information, or maybe developing a contingency plan? Make a list of these potential actions.

Exercise 3.3: Stress Busters for Difficult Decisions

<u>Step 1:</u> Find a peaceful space where you can breathe without disturbance. Deep, slow, intentional breathing can be your anchor amidst the stormy sea of stress.

<u>Step 2:</u> Visualize your stress as a formless entity floating above you. Ground yourself in the physical sensations of the here and now. Your stress is out there, disconnected from you.

<u>Step 3:</u> Identify the elements of the decision that are causing you stress. Write them down if you need to. Dissecting your stress helps you understand its components.

<u>Step 4:</u> Consider the stress components and identify which elements are within your control. For the elements that are beyond your control, practice the art of acceptance.

<u>Step 5:</u> Envision each possible outcome of your decision. Play through the scenarios in your mind, visualizing both success and failure. Preparation can often bring peace of mind.

<u>Step 6:</u> Remind yourself that you have the power to choose. This decision is in your hands. Embrace the autonomy and let it empower you.

<u>Step 7:</u> Finally, return to your breathing. Let the calm of the process wash over you. When you're ready, open your eyes, carrying this newfound calmness into your reality.

Exercise 3.4: Balancing The Buzz

Step 1: Start by acknowledging the excitement you are feeling. Write it down. Is it the thrill of a new job offer, the adventure of relocating to a new city, or the joy of adopting a pet? Naming the source of your excitement is the first step in managing it.

Step 2: Dive deeper into this emotion. What is it about this situation that's causing such a thrill? Is it the novelty, the challenge, or the potential reward? It's important to pinpoint what's causing the buzz to understand it better.

Step 3: Now, imagine the scenario once the initial excitement has faded. How will you feel then? This step helps you to look beyond the immediate rush of excitement and consider the long-term implications of your decision.

Step 4: On a sheet of paper, jot down the pros and cons of the decision. This exercise serves to engage your logical mind and might bring to light aspects you may have overlooked in your excitement.

Step 5: Pretend you're an advisor to a friend who's in your situation. What would you tell them? Often, we give others more balanced advice than we give ourselves.

Step 6: On a scale of 1 to 10, rate your excitement or anticipation. Do this before and after the exercise. Did your score change? It's not about lowering the score but understanding how rational thinking can alter the intensity of your emotions.

Step 7: Now that you've considered different aspects of your decision, it's time to make a choice. After deciding, reflect on how the process felt. How did engaging both your emotional and rational mind influence your decision?

Exercise 3.5: Confidence Calibration

Step 1: Identify the decision you are about to make. Write it down. Now, ask yourself, "Why am I confident about this decision?" Note down the reasons for your confidence.

Step 2: Consider each reason you've noted. Do they hold water? Are they based on sound reasoning, current information, and relevant experiences? Or are they just reflections of past successes? Be brutally honest with yourself.

Step 3: On a scale of 1 to 10, where would you place your current level of confidence? Write it down. This gives you a baseline for your confidence level.

Step 4: No one is infallible. Everyone makes mistakes. Write down some instances where you have made mistakes in the past, and remind yourself that it's okay to be wrong.

Step 5: Now, go back to your Confidence Meter. Has your rating changed after steps 3 and 4? If yes, note down the new rating.

Step 6: Identify the elements of the decision that are making you feel secure. Are they tangible, like a safety net or backup plan, or intangible, like a feeling of readiness or previous successes?

Step 7: Examine each element of security. Is it reliable and relevant in the current context of the decision? Modify your sense of security accordingly.

Step 8: Finally, based on your adjusted levels of confidence and security, revisit your decision. Do you need to gather more information, seek advice, or reassess your options? Plan your next steps accordingly.

Exercise 3.6: The Guilt and Regret Reconciliation Guide

<u>Step 1:</u> Pinpoint the emotion. Are you dealing with guilt or regret? Write down the decision you're wrestling with and connect the dots to your feelings. Accept these emotions, validate them, and understand they are part of the human experience.

<u>Step 2:</u> Remember the Drama Triangle? Let's apply it here. Are you placing yourself in the role of the Victim, Persecutor, or the Rescuer? Put pen to paper and spell it out. The objective here is to understand your position and see if it's facilitating guilt or regret.

<u>Step 3:</u> This step is about examining the root cause of your feelings. Why are you feeling guilty or regretful? Write down your thoughts. It's essential to get to the heart of the matter before you can move forward.

<u>Step 4:</u> Sometimes your emotions can lead you astray, so now it's time for a reality check. Question the authenticity of your guilt or regret. Are they a product of your own expectations or the expectations of others? Is your regret stemming from self-criticism or a growth mindset? Write down your findings.

<u>Step 5:</u> Guilt and regret can make you feel trapped, but there's a key to that cage and it's called self-forgiveness. Pen a forgiveness statement to yourself. Recognize the strength it takes to face difficult decisions, accept your humanness, and acknowledge that everyone makes mistakes.

<u>Step 6:</u> While it's not pleasant to feel guilt or regret, these emotions can be insightful teachers. Ask yourself, what can you learn from this? How can you apply this newfound knowledge to future decisions?

<u>Step 7:</u> Give it a day or two, then revisit your thoughts and emotions. Has there been a shift? Have your findings relieved some of the guilt or regret? How has your perspective on the situation changed?

Exercise 3.7: Sailing through the Sea of Relief

Step 1: Pinpoint the exact moment when you feel a sense of relief wash over you after making a decision. Can you describe it? Is it like a weight lifted off your chest, or a deep breath after holding it in for so long? Write down how you feel.

Step 2: Now, take a moment to truly enjoy this feeling. You've earned it! Close your eyes, take a deep breath, and let the relief fill you up. But, don't lose sight of why you're feeling this relief—it's a result of a decision you've made.

Step 3: Open your eyes and bring to mind the decision you've made. What led you to it? Were there any alternatives? Could there be any consequences, either immediate or delayed? Jot these down.

Step 4: Now, revisit the Drama Triangle from earlier chapters. With your decision and its potential consequences in mind, do you find yourself leaning towards any of the roles—Victim, Rescuer, or Persecutor? Be honest with yourself, there's no right or wrong answer here.

Step 5: Are you feeling overly confident about your decision in retrospect? Do you think it was 'obvious' or 'inevitable'? That's hindsight bias. Acknowledge it if it's there. It doesn't take away from your decision-making process, but it's essential to recognize it for what it is.

Step 6: Finally, based on your self-reflection, outline what steps you need to take next. This could be about mitigating potential fallout, planning for consequences, or even just celebrating your decision.

Step 7: Now, revisit that initial feeling of relief. Has it changed in any way? Is it still as intense, or has it mellowed down? This step helps you understand how reflection and planning can balance the highs of relief. Write down your observations.

Exercise 4.1: The Rational Decision-Making Model Worksheet

The Rational Decision-Making Model Worksheet

Step	Description	Questions to Ask	Professional Decision Example	Personal Decision Example
Identify the Problem	Recognize an issue that needs to be addressed.	What is the issue? Why does it need to be addressed?	Declining sales numbers in a product line.	Need to improve my physical fitness.
Analyze the Problem	Understand the underlying factors and constraints of the problem.	What are the underlying factors? What constraints exist?	Market saturation, changing consumer behavior.	Time constraints, lack of motivation.
Identify Decision Criteria	Establish the factors that will influence the decision.	What factors will impact the decision?	Cost, ROI, customer satisfaction.	Budget, time commitment, health goals.
Generate Alternatives	Develop different solutions or paths to address the problem.	What are the possible solutions?	Introduce a new product, rebrand, discount.	Join a gym, start running, take up swimming.
Evaluate Alternatives	Assess each alternative based on the decision criteria.	How does each alternative align with the criteria?	Analyzing profit potential for each option.	Comparing the cost and enjoyment of each option.
Select the Best Alternative	Choose the most suitable solution that aligns with the criteria.	Which solution best meets the criteria?	Launching a new product after thorough analysis.	Joining a gym with suitable timings and classes.
Implement the Decision	Put the selected alternative into action.	How will the decision be implemented?	Execute the new product launch plan.	Sign up for the gym, create a workout schedule.
Evaluate the Decision	Review the results and ensure the decision achieved the desired outcome.	Was the problem solved? What can be learned for the future?	Assess sales numbers, customer feedback.	Monitor fitness progress, adjust as needed.

Exercise 4.2: OODA Loop Worksheet

OODA Loop Worksheet				
Step	**Description**	**Questions to Ask**	**Professional Decision Example**	**Personal Decision Example**
Observe	Gather information from multiple sources to understand the situation.	What data is available? What are the key observations?	Monitoring market trends for product positioning.	Researching vacation destinations.
Orient	Analyze the information, understand the context, and align it with your experiences and goals.	What does the information mean? How does it relate to goals?	Identifying competitors' strengths and weaknesses.	Comparing climates, costs, and activities.
Decide	Based on your orientation, make a decision on the best course of action.	What are the options? What is the best decision right now?	Launching a new product to fill a market gap.	Choosing a beach vacation for relaxation.
Act	Implement the decision, monitor results, and prepare to loop back if necessary.	How will the decision be implemented? How will success be measured?	Execute the product launch plan, assess feedback.	Book the trip, pack appropriately, enjoy!

Exercise 4.3: Cynefin Decision-Making Framework Worksheet

Cynefin Decision-Making Framework Worksheet					
Domain	Description	Questions to Ask During Doubt	Actions to Move Towards Decision	Professional Decision Example	Personal Decision Example
Clear	Problem with clear cause and effect	Is the problem well-defined? Is there an established process?	Follow the best practice or procedure.	Standardizing a hiring process.	Following a budgeting plan.
Complicated	Problem requires expert analysis and multiple solutions exist	Does the problem require expert knowledge? Are there multiple solutions?	Analyze the problem and apply an expert solution.	Designing a complex supply chain.	Buying a house with specific requirements.
Complex	Problem is unpredictable and solutions emerge through understanding patterns	How are elements interconnected? How can a pattern be recognized?	Probe, sense, respond. Experiment to find solutions.	Introducing a new product in a diverse market.	Raising children in a multicultural environment.
Chaotic	Problem in chaos without clear relationships	What immediate actions can restore order? Is stability the priority?	Act, sense, respond. Implement immediate containment.	Responding to a major organizational crisis like a fire.	Handling a sudden family emergency.
Disorder	Uncertainty about which domain applies	What aspects of the problem are clear/ complicated/ complex/ chaotic?	Break down the problem, categorize, and respond accordingly.	Developing a strategy in a highly uncertain industry.	Making a career change without a clear path.

185

Exercise 4.4: Pareto Analysis Framework Worksheet

Pareto Analysis Framework Worksheet				
Step	**Description**	**Actions to Move Towards Decision**	**Professional Decision Example**	**Personal Decision Example**
Identify the Problem	Define the specific problem or issue you want to address.	Clearly state the problem.	Increasing customer satisfaction in a service-oriented business.	Improving personal time management.
List the Causes	Identify all potential causes of the problem.	Brainstorm and list all possible causes.	Analyzing reasons for customer complaints (e.g., slow service, product quality).	Identifying what takes up most of your time (e.g., tasks, distractions).
Score Each Cause	Assign scores to each cause based on its significance.	Evaluate and score each cause based on its impact.	Scoring customer complaints based on frequency and impact on overall satisfaction.	Scoring activities by how much time they consume.
Calculate the 80/20	Calculate which 20% of the causes are responsible for 80% of the problem.	Identify the key causes that make up the majority of the problem.	Identifying key areas responsible for most customer complaints, such as slow service.	Finding the few activities that consume the majority of your time.
Apply the Analysis	Focus on addressing the significant causes identified in the previous step.	Plan and implement solutions for the key causes.	Implementing solutions to address slow service, such as hiring more staff or improving training.	Reducing or optimizing the time spent on major activities identified.

Exercise 5.1: Sufficient Information Worksheet

Sufficient Information Worksheet

Step	Description	Actions to Determine Relevance and Right Amount	Professional Example (Market Entry Decision)	Personal Example (Choosing a School for Children)
Define the Objective	Identify what you're trying to achieve with the decision.	State the decision's main goal or purpose.	Determine if a new market is suitable for business expansion.	Decide on the best educational environment for children.
Identify Criteria	Determine the essential factors that will guide the decision.	List the most important factors or criteria.	Consider market size, competition, customer demand, legal regulations.	Evaluate curriculum, teacher quality, location, extracurriculars.
Gather Information	Collect relevant data, facts, and opinions from various sources.	Compile diverse information that aligns with the identified criteria.	Market research, competitor analysis, legal studies, customer feedback.	School visits, parent interviews, online reviews, educational experts.
Balance Information	Ensure the information is not too heavily reliant on one source or perspective.	Cross-check information from different sources for balance.	Consult industry reports, expert opinions, competitor insights.	Gather opinions from different parents, teachers, and students.
Filter Information	Remove unnecessary details and focus on what truly matters.	Filter information through the criteria to keep only what's essential.	Focus on relevant market dynamics, competitors, regulations.	Concentrate on school reputation, teaching quality, location.
Assess Credibility	Evaluate the trustworthiness of the information.	Verify the sources and assess their credibility.	Validate information through reputable business publications.	Check school accreditation, reputable reviews, expert opinions.
Decide on the Right Amount	Determine when you have enough relevant information without being overwhelmed.	Recognize when all criteria are addressed without excess.	Stop when all market factors are analyzed without redundancy.	Cease gathering when all key educational aspects are considered.
Reflect on the Information Gathered	Review the information and ensure alignment with the decision objective and criteria.	Reflect on how the information supports the decision-making.	Analyze how market information aligns with business goals.	Reflect on how school information aligns with children's needs.

187

Exercise 5.2: Credibility Checker

Credibility Checker			
Source	Criteria for Evaluation	Actions to Assess Credibility	Example: Assessing Credibility
Technology	Verify the algorithms, data sources, and methodology behind the information.	Check for transparency in algorithms, data collection, and analysis.	Confirming the algorithm's process in a financial tech tool.
Internet	Check the domain, author, publication date, references, and the website's mission and contact information.	Look for reputable domains, peer-reviewed content, transparent authorship, and clear referencing.	Evaluating a health article on a well-known medical website.
Social Media	Investigate the author's background, the context of the post, any linked references, and reader comments.	Assess the author's qualifications, verify linked sources, analyze context and reader reactions.	Reviewing a product recommendation by a recognized industry influencer.
Mentors/Coaches	Examine the credentials, experience, and references of the person providing information.	Validate their qualifications, seek feedback from previous clients, observe their approach to mentoring.	Checking a business coach's track record and client testimonials.
Published Content	Look for a reputable publisher, author qualifications, cited sources, peer reviews, and consistency in information.	Verify publisher reputation, author's academic credentials, and the quality of cited sources.	Analyzing a scientific paper published in a renowned journal.
Rumors	Identify the original source of the rumor, if possible, and cross-check with reputable sources.	Seek evidence from reliable sources, investigate the origin, and be skeptical of unverified information.	Cross-referencing a celebrity rumor with reputable news agencies.
Biased Opinions	Recognize the potential biases, consider the context, and compare with other perspectives.	Identify underlying biases, assess the motive behind the opinion, compare with diverse viewpoints.	Understanding political bias in an opinion piece and comparing it with others.

Exercise 6.1: Bias Checker

<u>Step 1:</u> Quickly list the facts and evidence you are using to make this decision. Are you relying on stereotypes, assumptions, or previous experiences that may not apply to this specific situation? Focus on concrete evidence and try to filter out any subjective opinions.

<u>Step 2:</u> Think of a person or situation that is entirely different from the one you are currently dealing with. How would you approach this decision if the circumstances were different? Comparing and contrasting can shed light on hidden biases by revealing inconsistencies in your approach.

<u>Step 3:</u> Imagine explaining your decision-making process to a neutral third party. How would you justify your decision? If you find yourself struggling to explain without using subjective language, it may signal a bias.

<u>Step 4:</u> If possible, quickly consult with a friend or colleague, without giving your opinion first. Sometimes, an outside perspective can provide a valuable reality check.

<u>Step 5:</u> Do you have strong feelings or preferences that could be influencing your decision? If you feel strongly attached to one option, explore why that might be. An emotional attachment might indicate a bias.

<u>Step 6:</u> Review your thoughts and the evidence you have gathered. Have you identified any biases? If so, take a moment to reevaluate your possibility without them.

<u>Step 7:</u> Proceed with locking the possibility in, now with the increased awareness of potential biases and a more objective perspective.

Exercise 6.2: Creative Possibilities

Design thinking is a human-centered approach that encourages you to think creatively and empathetically to solve problems. Applying design thinking to decision-making helps you create more innovative possibilities and solutions.

<u>Step 1:</u> Empathize; understand the context, the people involved, and the emotional implications.

- Who is affected by this decision?
- What are their needs, desires, and pain points?
- How might they feel about various outcomes?
- What cultural, social, or economic factors might influence their perspectives?
- How can I best empathize with different stakeholders?

<u>Step 2:</u> Clearly articulate the problem or decision you are facing.

- What is the core problem or decision I am facing?
- How can I frame it in a way that is actionable?
- What are the constraints and limitations?
- What are the goals or desired outcomes?

<u>Step 3:</u> Brainstorm all possible options without judgment. (check the next exercises on mind mapping and brainstorming for more techniques)

- What are all the possible solutions or paths I can take?
- How can I encourage creative thinking and avoid judgment?
- What tools or methods might help facilitate brainstorming?
- How can I ensure diverse perspectives are considered?

<u>Step 4:</u> Create tangible representations of some of the ideas.

- What prototypes can represent the ideas or options?
- How can I make these prototypes tangible and testable?
- What resources do I need to create these prototypes?

<u>Step 5</u>: Evaluate the prototypes to gain insights.

- How can I test these prototypes?
- What criteria will I use to evaluate them?
- Who should be involved in testing, and how will I gather their feedback?
- What insights can I gain from this testing phase?

<u>Step 6</u>: Reflect on what you've learned and decide how to proceed.

- What did I learn from testing the prototypes?
- How do these insights inform my decision-making process?
- What are the pros and cons of each option?
- How do these options align with my values and goals?

<u>Step 7</u>: Make your decision and put it into action.

- What steps must I take to implement this decision?
- Who needs to be involved or informed?
- What resources or support are required?
- How will I monitor progress and make adjustments as needed?

<u>Step 8</u>: Assess the results and make any necessary adjustments.

- What were the outcomes of this decision?
- What went well, and what could have been done differently?
- What adjustments or next steps are necessary?
- How can I apply these insights to future decisions?

Exercise 6.3: Mind Mapping Guide

Think of mind mapping as a painting where your thoughts, ideas, and connections all come together to form a beautiful masterpiece. Here is a step-by-step guide to help you harness this creative tool, whether you're working on a new business plan or figuring out your next educational move.

<u>Step 1:</u> Begin by pinpointing the core idea or question you want to explore. This will be the sun in the center of your solar system, and everything else will orbit around it. Write it down in the center of your paper or digital platform. It's the seed from which everything else will grow, so make it something meaningful and focused.

<u>Step 2:</u> From the central theme, draw branches representing the primary topics or questions related to your main idea. Think of these as the main roads leading from a city center; they'll guide you to fascinating new places and insights.

<u>Step 3:</u> Sub-branches are where your main ideas break down into more specific elements. These could be facts, arguments, questions, or any detailed information. Consider them the charming alleyways and hidden gems off the main roads that lead to discovery and understanding.

<u>Step 4:</u> Engage your creative side by using colors, images, or symbols that resonate with the ideas. Think of them as spices in a dish; they add flavor, make it more engaging, and can help with memory and understanding.

<u>Step 5:</u> Look for connections between different branches and sub-branches. Draw lines or use arrows to show these relationships. It's like finding secret passages between rooms; they might reveal surprising connections and insights.

<u>Step 6:</u> Allow your mind map to evolve and grow organically. Don't be afraid to add new branches or rearrange things as new insights emerge. Your mind map is a living garden; it can grow and change as you cultivate it.

<u>Step 7:</u> Take a step back and look at the whole map. What patterns, insights, or surprises do you see? It's like standing on a hilltop, looking down at the landscape you've traversed, and appreciating the journey.

<u>Step 8:</u> If your mind map was an exploration, now it's time to chart a course. Identify the most potent ideas and insights, and turn them into actionable steps or plans. This is where you set sail, using the map to navigate towards your goals.

<u>Step 9 (Optional):</u> If it's a team effort, don't hesitate to share the mind map with others. Invite them to add, question, or explore. It's a communal garden, and others might plant seeds you never considered.

Exercise 6.4: Brainstorming Guide

<u>Step 1</u>: Start by pinpointing the exact problem or question you're trying to solve. Imagine you're setting the stage for a grand adventure; this is where you mark the starting point. Whether you're working on launching a new product or planning a family vacation, you must know precisely what you're looking to achieve. It's like setting the destination on your GPS; without it, you might end up lost.

<u>Step 2</u>: Bring together a group of people who can contribute various perspectives to the brainstorming session. It's not just about filling a room with people but finding those who can add real value to the discussion. Think of it as inviting guests to a dinner party - you want a mix of personalities and expertise to ensure lively and engaging conversation.

<u>Step 3</u>: Build a space where everyone feels comfortable expressing their ideas, no matter how wild or unconventional. Encourage a judgment-free zone where every thought is welcomed like a guest at a feast. If people feel hesitant, remind them that there are no wrong answers in brainstorming; it's about exploration and discovery.

<u>Step 4</u>: Sometimes, the creative engine needs a little priming. Start with a simple, fun exercise that gets people relaxed and engaged. Think of this like stretching before a run; it helps to loosen up and prepare for the main event.

<u>Step 5</u>: Now comes the exciting part. Let the ideas flow freely. Encourage participants to build on each other's thoughts, and don't be afraid to follow tangents. Sometimes the most unexpected paths lead to the most exciting destinations. This is the heart of the brainstorming session, where creativity meets possibility.

<u>Step 6</u>: Whether on a whiteboard, sticky notes, or a digital platform, make sure you capture every idea. They are like pieces of a puzzle, and you never know which one will fit perfectly into the solution you're seeking.

Step 7: Once the ideas are out there, it's time to sift through them and find the gems. Look for themes, connections, and patterns. Think of yourself as a treasure hunter, looking for the pieces of gold that resonate most with the problem at hand.

Step 8: Select the ideas that stand out and seem most promising. Start building a roadmap, turning those creative sparks into actionable steps. It's like taking the ingredients from a bustling market and forming a recipe to create a delicious meal.

Step 9: Reflect on the process, acknowledge the creativity and contributions, and celebrate the ideas generated. Remember, even if the perfect solution hasn't been found yet, the journey itself holds value and learning.

Step 10: Don't let the energy of the session fade away. Assign responsibilities, set timelines, and ensure that the brainstorming session is not just a creative burst but a launching pad for real action.

Exercise 6.5: How comfortable are you?

This reflective exercise is designed to help you determine your tendency to remain in your comfort zone. There are no right or wrong answers here. The purpose of this exercise is to gain insight into your own tendencies and behaviors, and to identify areas where you might be able to push yourself beyond your comfort zone for growth and development. Grab your notebook, find a quiet place, and take a few moments to deeply breathe and reflect.

Step 1: Write down your daily routine for the last week, noting the activities you did, the people you interacted with, the places you went. Try to be as detailed as possible.

Step 2: Analyze your routine. Were there moments where you felt uncomfortable or challenged, or was everything relatively familiar and safe? List down activities or situations where you felt at ease and those where you felt any discomfort.

Step 3: Think about the last time you actively tried something new or different. It could be anything from trying a new cuisine to adopting a new habit or learning a new skill. How did you feel before, during, and after the experience?

Step 4: Reflect on how you generally react to unexpected changes or challenges. Are you quickly adaptive, or do you resist and try to keep things the same?

Step 5: Identify areas of your life where you want to grow or improve. What steps have you taken in the past to work on these areas? How does your comfort zone limit you in these areas?

Step 6: Think about one small step you could take towards expanding your comfort zone in an area you've identified for growth. How might you begin to stretch yourself in that area this week?

Exercise 7.1: Applying the IVIC Model

IVIC Model Self-Coaching Tool		
Pillar	**Key Questions for Personal Decisions**	**Key Questions for Professional Decisions**
Identity	- Which choice aligns with my values and beliefs? - What does this decision say about who I am? - How does this reflect my passions and abilities?	- How does this decision align with my professional values and career goals? - What does this say about my professional persona? - How does this choice reflect my strengths and skills in the workplace?
Vision	- Does this align with my long-term life goals? - How does this choice fit into my vision for my future? - What do I hope to achieve with this decision?	- How does this decision fit into the larger picture of my career trajectory? - What are the potential long-term effects on my professional growth? - How does this align with the organization's goals?
Impact	- How will this decision affect those around me? - What positive change could come from this choice? - How does this decision resonate with my desire to make a difference?	- What will be the impact of this decision on my team and organization? - How can this choice contribute to overall success and innovation? - What change can I drive within my professional sphere with this decision?
Cost	- What trade-offs must I make for this decision? - Can I afford this choice financially, emotionally, and time-wise? - What might I gain or lose with this decision?	- What are the potential risks and benefits of this choice in a professional context? - How does this decision align with the resources available? - What might be the financial implications, and am I prepared to handle them?

Exercise 8.1: Societal impact on belief system formation

1. What do I believe in? *(think of core beliefs like religious, world-view, and self-image related beliefs)*

2. Why do I hold these beliefs? *(state the factual arguments and evidence that support these beliefs)*

3. How did I develop these beliefs? *(mention the sources of how you learned the factual arguments and reached the evidence that support these beliefs)*

4. Have these beliefs changed over time? *(write down the reasons for your yes/no)*

5. Are your beliefs based on evidence, personal experiences, or critical thinking? *(evaluate the answers you gave to questions 2, 3, and 4)*

6. Have I explored alternative viewpoints or considered different perspectives? *(write down the reasons for your yes/no)*

7. Was I able to articulate the reasons behind my beliefs? *(yes/no)*

Exercise 8.2: Motive Mapping

<u>Step 1:</u> Take a moment to think about your goals. The big ones, the small ones, those that are immediate and those that are in the distant future. Write them down. It could be a career milestone, a personal ambition, a financial target, or even a simple everyday task.

<u>Step 2:</u> For each goal, write down why you want to achieve it. What drives you towards this goal? Be honest and patient with yourself. The first answers that come up might not be the truest ones. Dig deeper. *(refer to the different motives I mentioned in the previous paragraphs)*

<u>Step 3:</u> With your motives listed down, identify whether they are intrinsic or extrinsic. Does the satisfaction come from within, or is it tied to an external reward or recognition?

<u>Step 4:</u> Now, consider your belief system. Are these motives aligned with your authentic self? Do they resonate with your core values and beliefs? Or are they shaped by societal norms or the expectations of others? Be brutally honest with yourself here.

<u>Step 5:</u> This step might require you to take a break. Give yourself time to absorb the insights you've uncovered. Reflect on them, and if necessary, reevaluate your goals based on your authentic motives.

<u>Step 6:</u> Repeat. Motives might change as you grow and evolve. So, make it a habit to revisit this exercise at different stages of your life.

Exercise 8.3: Your Values

<u>Step 1:</u> Identify the times when you were happiest. Find examples from both your career and personal life. This will ensure some balance in your answers.

1. What were you doing?
2. Were you with other people? Who?
3. What other factors contributed to your happiness?

<u>Step 2:</u> Identify the times when you were most proud. Use examples from your career and personal life.

1. Why were you proud?
2. Did other people share your pride? Who?
3. What other factors contributed to your feelings of pride?

<u>Step 3:</u> Identify the times when you were most fulfilled and satisfied. Use both work and personal examples.

1. What need or desire was fulfilled?
2. How and why did the experience give your life meaning?
3. What other factors contributed to your feelings of fulfillment?

<u>Step 4:</u> Determine your top values, based on your experiences of happiness, pride, and fulfillment. Why is each experience truly important and memorable?

Use the following list of common personal values to help you get started – and aim for about 10 top values. As you work through, you may find that some of these naturally combine. For instance, if you value philanthropy, community, and generosity, you might say that service to others is one of your top values.

Grounding Values *Our most basic, fundamental views of the world.*	• Affection • Curiosity • Food and Shelter • Kindness • Maintenance • Obedience	• Physical Functioning • Self-Restraint • Sensuality • Wonder • Safety
Family *Our fundamental relationships to ourselves and to others.*	• Belief • Belonging • Caretaking • Discipline • Duty • Economic Security • Fairness • Honesty • Legacy	• Loyalty • Patience • Playfulness • Recognition • Respect • Self-Sacrifice • Self-Worth • Stability • Tradition
Management *Establishing and maintaining stability in our lives.*	• Achievement • Authority • Charity • Competence • Competition • Decisiveness • Efficiency • Financial Success • Hierarchical Ability • Informing • Managing	• Order • Patriotism • Predictability • Problem Solving • Productivity • Quality • Rationality • Recreation • Responsibility • Rule of Law • Self Confidence
Relational Awareness *Individual responsibility for developing yourself and determining the quality of relationships with others.*	• Acceptance • Analogy • Balance • Being Present • Choice • Commitment • Courage • Creativity • Diversity • Empathy • Independence	• Intimacy • Learning • Listening • Openness • Personal Growth • Questioning • Reflection • Risk • Search For Meaning • Trust • Wellbeing
Systems Awareness *How you interact within the context of groups and society at large.*	• Beauty • Collaboration • Community • Development • Dialogue • Empowering Others • Equality • Exploration • Strategy	• Flexibility • Innovation • Integrity • Interdependence • Intuition • Partnership • Service • Simultaneity • Sustainability
Expansion *Future-oriented aspirations and goals.*	• Altruism • Detachment • Global Enfranchisement • Human Rights • Inspiring Others • Mind-Body Integration	• Nonviolence • Planetary Ecology • Reconciliation • Simplification • Spirituality

Exercise 9.1: The Genetic Roots of Passion

<u>Step 1:</u> Draw up a family tree and list any interests, hobbies, or professions you know each member is or was passionate about. This could include your parents, grandparents, and even great-grandparents if possible.

<u>Step 2:</u> Look for patterns or similarities between your passions and those of your family members. Do you find that your interests align with theirs, even if it's in a general sense, like a shared love for the arts, sports, sciences, or humanitarian causes?

<u>Step 3:</u> Reflect on whether these passions were inherited or influenced. Did you grow up in an environment that encouraged these passions, or did you naturally gravitate towards them, even if they were not part of your immediate environment?

<u>Step 4:</u> Consider if you have any natural abilities or skills that align with your passions and if these traits can be observed in other family members. These could suggest a possible genetic component.

<u>Step 5:</u> If possible, have a discussion with your family members about their passions and see if they believe there's a genetic component to their interests.

Exercise 9.2: Finding your passion

Have you seen Jim Carry's "Yes Man"? Or Bradly Cooper's "Limitless"? This is similar to what you need to do to discover your passions. You simply need to get yourself out there in the world and explore things!

<u>Step 1:</u> Start by making a list of things that intrigue you. These could be anything from activities you enjoy, topics you like reading or learning about, or dreams you've always had. Don't limit yourself at this stage, just write down anything that comes to mind.

<u>Step 2:</u> Choose one or two areas from your list that resonate with you the most. Now, make a plan to explore these areas in more depth. Depending on your preference, this could involve:

- Reading books
- Watching videos
- Taking classes
- Speaking with experts in the field.

The aim is to give your brain plenty of exposure to this area, which can help stimulate your interest and deepen your connection with the subject.

<u>Step 3:</u> Mindfulness is a powerful way to heighten your awareness and engagement with the activity you're trying to cultivate a passion for.

Whether you're reading, learning, or doing something related to your area of interest, try to do it mindfully. This means paying full attention to the activity, engaging in it completely, and noticing all the sensations, emotions, and thoughts it evokes in you. This practice can strengthen the neural pathways in your brain associated with this activity and enhance your emotional connection with it.

<u>Step 4:</u> Setting achievable goals related to your passion can help increase your motivation to engage in the activity. This, in turn, will stimulate your brain's reward system, creating a positive feedback loop that encourages you to keep going. So, creating a vivid vision of what pursuing your passion would look like will help increase your motivation and keep you focused.

<u>Step 5:</u> Consistency is key. Spend time engaging in or learning about your chosen interest. Neuroplasticity relies on regular stimulation and practice. The more frequently you engage with the activity, the stronger those neural pathways will become, and the easier it will be for your brain to engage with the activity. Avoid quick judgements, and give yourself a chance to truly explore.

<u>Step 6:</u> Keep track of your progress. Reflect on how your relationship with the activity has evolved, what you've learned, and how you feel when you're engaged in it. Recognizing your progress will stimulate your brain's reward system, increasing feelings of pleasure and satisfaction, which can further fuel your passion.

Exercise 9.3: Liberating your passion

You might have already explored the world, but there is a limiting belief anchoring down the passions you have discovered, and preventing you from setting sail freely after your passion. Find a quiet and comfortable space where you can reflect without interruptions. Take a few deep breaths to center yourself and create a calm state of mind.

<u>Step 1:</u> Begin by reflecting on areas of your life where you feel a deep sense of joy, excitement, and fulfillment. Consider activities, subjects, or interests that have consistently sparked your curiosity and enthusiasm. Ask yourself:

- What activities do I naturally gravitate towards in my free time?
- When do I feel most energized and alive?
- Are there any hobbies or interests that I have always been drawn to?
- What activities make time fly by effortlessly?

<u>Step 2:</u> Reflect on any limiting beliefs or self-doubts that may be holding you back from pursuing your passion or fully embracing it. These beliefs might include thoughts like "I'm not talented enough," "It's too late to start," or "I'll never be successful." Identify and write down the specific limiting beliefs that come to mind.

<u>Step 3:</u> Challenging your limiting beliefs: Take each limiting belief you identified and examine the evidence for and against it. Ask yourself:

- Is there any concrete evidence that supports this belief? Is it based on facts or assumptions?
- Can I think of any counterexamples or instances where this belief might not hold true?
- How might my life be different if I didn't hold onto this belief?

<u>Step 4:</u> Once you have challenged your limiting beliefs, reframe them into more empowering and supportive statements. Replace them with positive and affirming beliefs that encourage you to pursue your passion. For example, if your limiting belief is "I'm not talented enough," you could reframe it as "I have a unique perspective and valuable skills to contribute."

<u>Step 5</u>: Reflect on your commitment to overcoming your limiting beliefs and pursuing your passion. Ask yourself:

- How important is it for me to overcome these limiting beliefs?
- What steps am I willing to take to challenge and let go of these beliefs?
- Am I ready to embrace a new perspective that empowers me to pursue my passion?

<u>Step 6</u>: Creating an action plan: Identify specific actions you can take to nurture and pursue your passion, despite your limiting beliefs. Break them down into small, manageable steps. I would encourage you to:

- Seek support from mentors
- Taking courses or workshops
- Dedicate regular time to engage in activities related to your passion.

If you already have a passion and your limiting beliefs are holding you down, the above tools will play a role in guiding your steps and providing you with the confidence and confirmation you need to move forward passionately.

<u>Step 7</u>: Use this journal as a tool to document your progress, track your growth, and revisit your reflections whenever you need a reminder of your commitment.

<u>Step 8</u>: Share your reflections and action plan with a trusted friend, family member, or mentor who can support you on your journey. Discuss your goals, challenges, and progress, and ask for their encouragement and guidance when needed.

Exercise 9.4: Is your passion influenced?

Step 1: Draw a timeline of your life from birth to the present day. Mark on this timeline all the significant moments that have made an impact on your interests or passions. These could include family trips, educational experiences, influential people, or impactful events.

Step 2: For each significant moment on your timeline, identify the environment or situation in which it took place. Ask yourself, "What about this environment led to the interest or passion I developed?"

Step 3: Look for patterns and themes in these moments.
- Are there common elements that keep showing up? What are these?
- Are they related to particular environments or types of environments? What are these environments?

Step 4: Reflect on the cultural environment you grew up in.
- What activities or pursuits did your culture value?
- How did this affect your interests?

Step 5: Think about the professional or educational environments you've been in. What opportunities were available to you in these environments that shaped your interests?

Step 6: How has the era you're living in shaped your interests? Have certain technologies or societal trends influenced what you're passionate about?

Exercise 9.5: Discovering your talent

This exercise can take up to a month to finish, so stay dedicated and focused. It will also combine your journeys of finding talent and passion into one. Discovering your talents is a journey, so be patient with yourself and enjoy the process. It is totally okay if you look like an idiot. Actually, I encourage you to be so. Ask stupid questions, be curious, and do not be shy to try out whatever you feel you want to.

Step 1: Over a period of one month, engage in at least 10 new activities. These could be anything from drawing, writing, dancing, programming, cooking, debating, etc. It is important that you throw yourself into whatever you have not tried enough before, even if it does not seem interesting in the beginning. You will never know how good you are until you actually try.

Step 2: After each activity, write a journal entry detailing your experience, feelings, and interest in the activity. Ask yourself:
- How did I feel while doing this activity?
- Did time fly by or did it feel like a chore?
- Did I feel a sense of joy or fulfillment?
- What activities or tasks feel effortless to me?
- What actions do I perform that others seem to struggle with?
- Have I found an activity/task that I both enjoy and seem to be good at?

Step 3: Reflect on comments or feedback from others. Ask yourself:
- When have people complimented my skills or noted my natural aptitude?
- What activities did I enjoy the most?
- Were there activities I was naturally good at?
- What patterns do I see in the activities that I enjoyed and excelled in?
- When have others noted that I excel in certain areas?
- Have there been consistent compliments or observations across different areas of my life?

<u>Step 4</u>: Show your work, share your experiences with friends, family, teachers or mentors. Ask for their honest opinion on where they think your talents lie. Afterwards, ask yourself:

- What feedback did I receive that resonates with my own feelings about my strengths?
- Were there any surprising observations made by others?

<u>Step 5</u>: Choose one or two activities that you enjoyed and seemed naturally good at, and spend the next month honing your skills in these areas. Set yourself challenges and push your boundaries. Along the way, ask yourself:

- How much have I improved since I started?
- Do I still enjoy this activity even when it's challenging?

<u>Step 6</u>: After the period of deliberate practice, review your progress. Think about whether you'd like to continue in this activity or explore something new. Ask yourself:

- Did I feel a sense of progress and accomplishment?
- Do I see myself continuing with this activity in the long term?

Exercise 10.1: Crafting Your Life's Mission

<u>Step 1</u>: Recall the four elements of Ikigai: what you love, what you are good at, what the world needs, and what you can be paid for. Think about how these resonate with you.
- What are you passionate about?
- What are you good at?
- What does the world need?
- What can you be paid for?

<u>Step 2</u>: Examine where these elements intersect in your life. Recognize your passion's influence on your profession, mission, and vocation.
- How does your passion intersect with your profession?
- Where does your passion meet the world's needs?

<u>Step 3</u>: Look at the convergence of all four aspects. This meeting point embodies your Ikigai or unique purpose.
- What emerges when all four aspects converge?
- How does this center reflect your life's mission?

<u>Step 4</u>: Put your Ikigai into words. Craft a statement that represents your values, passions, and how they meet the world's needs.
- How can you articulate your Ikigai in a sentence?
- How does it reflect what the world needs?

<u>Step 5</u>: Establish short-term and long-term goals that align with your Ikigai.
- What goals resonate with your Ikigai?
- How will these goals help you fulfill your purpose?

<u>Step 6</u>: Share your mission statement with trusted individuals to gain insights and perspectives.
- How do others perceive your mission?
- Do they see alignment between your Ikigai and your life?

<u>Step 7</u>: Incorporate your mission into your daily life. Keep it visible and refer to it regularly.
- How can you embody your mission every day?
- How will you remind yourself of your Ikigai?

Exercise 11.1: Decision Tree

Decision Tree

Step	Description	Personal Example	Professional Example
Identify Decision & Objectives	Define what you're trying to decide and what your main objectives are.	Choosing between a beach or mountain vacation considering factors like family preferences, budget, weather.	Deciding between two suppliers for your business, based on factors like reliability, cost, contract terms.
Start Building the Tree	Draw branches for each possible alternative.	Draw a tree that starts with the two vacation options: beach or mountains.	Start with two branches for Supplier A and Supplier B.
Identify Possible Outcomes	Create sub-branches for different scenarios or outcomes for each alternative.	Under the "Beach" branch, include outcomes like "Sunny" or "Rainy."	For each supplier, add sub-branches for "Reliable" or "Unreliable."
Analyze Potential Repercussions	Think about the potential effects your decision might have on people, nature, or other factors.	Consider how the weather would impact family enjoyment.	Analyze how a supplier's reliability might affect company profit and reputation.

Exercise 11.2: Giving Back

Find a quiet and comfortable space where you can reflect without distractions. Take a few deep breaths to center yourself and create a sense of calm. When you have your notebook ready, and you feel well concentrated, start the exercise.

Step 1: Begin by reflecting on the help and support you have received from others throughout your life. Consider both significant acts of kindness and small gestures that have made a difference. Take a moment to express genuine gratitude for each of these instances. Think about:

- Who are the people that have provided significant support and assistance in your life?
- What specific acts of kindness or support have you received from these individuals?
- How have these acts impacted your journey or helped you overcome challenges?
- In what ways have these individuals influenced your personal growth or development?

Step 2: Write down a list of the people who have had a positive impact on your life. Include family members, friends, mentors, teachers, colleagues, or even strangers who have shown you kindness. Reflect on how their assistance or presence has shaped your journey.

- Who are the individuals that come to mind when you think about those who have had a positive impact on your life?
- Can you identify different categories of people, such as family, friends, mentors, teachers, colleagues, or strangers?
- What specific instances or qualities of each person have shaped your journey in a positive way?
- How have these individuals contributed to your personal, professional, or emotional well-being?

<u>Step 3:</u> Contemplate the opportunities you have to reciprocate and give back to others. Consider the skills, knowledge, resources, or unique qualities you possess that can be of service to those around you or the broader community.

- What unique talents, skills, or resources do you possess that can be of service to others?
- In what ways can you utilize these qualities to make a positive impact on those around you?
- Are there specific causes, organizations, or communities that resonate with you and align with your passion?
- How can you incorporate acts of kindness, generosity, or support into your daily life or routines?

Exercise 12.1: Decision Cost Analysis

<u>Step 1:</u> Write down the decision you're facing and list the options you're considering, maybe you are trying to choose between buying a new car or continuing with public transportation, or you are between investing in a new product line or improving the existing ones.

<u>Step 2</u>: For each option, identify the risks or what you might "choose to lose."

Option	Risk Description	Personal Example	Professional Example
Option A	Describe the potential risks.	Risk of monthly car payments and maintenance.	Risk of failure in a new, untested market.
Option B	Describe the potential risks.	Risk of less convenience with public transport.	Risk of stagnation with existing products.

<u>Step 3</u>: For each identified risk, assess the probability (likelihood) and impact (severity) on a scale of 1-5, with 5 being the highest.

Risk	Probability (1-5)	Impact (1-5)	Personal Example	Professional Example
Risk from Option A	Rate the likelihood.	Rate the severity.	Probability: 3, Impact: 4 (car maintenance)	Probability: 2, Impact: 5 (market failure)
Risk from Option B	Rate the likelihood.	Rate the severity.	Probability: 4, Impact: 2 (public transport)	Probability: 4, Impact: 3 (product stagnation)

<u>Step 4:</u> Multiply the probability by the impact for each risk to get a risk score.

Personal Example: Risk Score for Option A = 3 (Probability) × 4 (Impact) = 12
Professional Example: Risk Score for Option B = 4 (Probability) × 3 (Impact) = 12

<u>Step 5:</u> Compare the risk scores for each option. The option with the lower score may represent the lower risk, but consider all factors, including potential benefits.

Personal Example: Weighing the convenience of owning a car against the costs.
Professional Example: Balancing the opportunity for growth with the potential for loss.

Exercise 13.1: Life Direction Introspection

Step 1: Take a few moments to reflect on where you are in your life right now. What are the things you are currently pursuing? It could be a career, an education, a hobby, a relationship, or personal growth. Write these down in as much detail as possible.

Step 2: Think back to the times in your life when you've changed direction. It could be a job switch, a change in educational fields, or even shifts in personal relationships or hobbies. Write down these instances and try to remember why you made those changes. Was it due to a change in interests, circumstances, or insights? What was the outcome of these changes?

Step 3: Now, analyze whether you have a direction at the moment. Do you have a clear goal or an objective you are striving for, or do you feel like you're drifting aimlessly? If you find a definite direction, write it down. If you find yourself drifting, acknowledge this fact without judgment.

Step 4: For both past changes in direction and your current path (or lack thereof), reflect on your feelings of satisfaction, fulfillment, and happiness. Did the changes lead to more satisfaction or less? How do you feel about your current direction or lack of it?

Exercise 13.2: Setting an inclusive plan

This exercise is designed to help you create a comprehensive map of your journey towards your envisioned decision, examining the specific steps you'll take, their interconnectedness, and the expected outcomes.

<u>Step1:</u> Begin with visualizing your ultimate goal. Write down one main goal for each area. I would suggest for the following steps that you finish the whole exercise for one goal, and then move on to the next one to maintain your focus.

<u>Step 2:</u> Now, break the goal into smaller tasks that you must complete to achieve your goal.

<u>Step 3:</u> Dive into each task, breaking it down into smaller, manageable steps.

- What specifically does each task involve?
- What is the expected outcome of each task?
- How does each task contribute to the overall phase and eventually, to your goals?
- Why have you chosen this particular task? What alternatives did you consider?
- Does the sequence of tasks within each phase make sense? Is there a more efficient way to order them?
- What is the timeline for each task to be completed, so that you can achieve the goal on time?

<u>Step 4:</u> After going through each task, look at your overall plan.

- Do these phases logically lead you towards your goals?
- Are there any gaps or redundant steps?
- How does each phase transition into the next?
- Adjust your plan as needed until you're confident about it.

Exercise 13.3: Feasibility Audit

<u>Step 1:</u> Look at each task you've identified in the previous exercise, and identify the resources you'll need for each task. These could include time, money, skills, equipment, or emotional support.

- What resources do you already have?
- What resources do you need to acquire?
- How can you realistically obtain these resources?

<u>Step 2:</u> Assess each phase in your plan.

- Do you have enough resources to complete the tasks in this phase?
- If not, what alternatives could you consider? Could you reorder the tasks, or change them slightly, to make them more feasible with the resources you have?

<u>Step 3:</u> Reflect on the overall feasibility of your plan.

- Are there any parts of your plan that currently seem unattainable?
- What steps could you take to make them more achievable?
- Are there any tasks you could delegate or outsource?

<u>Step 4:</u> Make necessary adjustments to ensure your plan is feasible with the resources you have or can obtain.

Exercise 13.4: Risk Assessment and Contingency Planning

Do you anticipate potential obstacles, and have a plan for them so they don't derail your journey? Let's make sure you do.

<u>Step 1:</u> Revisit each task in your plan and think about the potential risks or obstacles that might arise.

- What could go wrong?
- How likely is it that this will happen?
- How would this affect your ability to complete the task and progress in your plan?

<u>Step 2:</u> For each identified risk, create a contingency plan.

- What steps could you take to mitigate this risk?
- If the risk does occur, how could you adapt your plan to keep moving forward?
- Could you leverage any resources or support to overcome this obstacle?

<u>Step 3:</u> Reflect on your overall plan with these contingency plans in mind.

- Do these plans make you feel more prepared for the journey ahead?
- Are there any risks you feel unequipped to handle?
- What additional resources or support could you leverage to better prepare for these risks?

<u>Step 4:</u> Adjust your plan as necessary to account for these contingency plans.

Exercise 13.5: Evidence-Based Confidence Building

Did you know that "FEAR" stands for "False Evidence Appearing Real"? Having real evidence helps you draw confidence that your plan will work. This could be your own past experiences, or examples from others who have successfully achieved similar goals. Let's have clarity on these evidences:

Step 1: Reflect on your own past achievements.
- What were some of the challenges you faced, and how did you overcome them?
- What strengths or strategies helped you succeed?
- How can these learnings apply to your new plan?

Step 2: Look for stories of people who have achieved similar goals to yours.
- How did they overcome obstacles and reach their goals?
- What can you learn from their experiences?

Step 3: Reflect on your plan in light of these insights.
- How does your plan align with the strategies and attitudes that helped you and others succeed in the past?
- Are there any changes you could make to your plan to better incorporate these lessons?

Exercise 13.6: Self-Image Enhancement Exercise

Step 1: Make a list of your skills, strengths, and accomplishments.
- What unique abilities do you bring to your plan?
- What achievements are you most proud of?

Step 2: Reflect on each task in your plan.
- How can your skills and strengths help you succeed in each task?
- How can your past accomplishments inspire confidence in your ability to achieve future goals?

Step 3: Develop positive affirmations based on your skills, strengths, and accomplishments.
- What encouraging words can you tell yourself when you face challenges?
- How can you remind yourself of your past successes and capabilities?

Step 4: Integrate these affirmations into your daily routine. Practice them especially when you need a confidence boost.

Exercise 13.7: Setting Boundaries

<u>Step 1</u>: Understand what matters most to you and where you might need boundaries. Ask yourself:

- What values are most important to me?
- In what situations do I feel drained or uncomfortable?
- What energizes me, and what do I want more of in my life?

<u>Step 2</u>: Translate your reflections into clear and actionable boundaries. Ask yourself:

- What specific boundary will honor my values and well-being in this area?
- How can I express this boundary empathetically?

Craft Clear Statements. For example, if work-life balance is crucial, your statement might be, "I will not check work emails after 6 PM to maintain quality family time."

<u>Step 3</u>: Learn to articulate these boundaries to others. Ask yourself:

- How will I communicate this boundary?
- Who needs to know about it?
- What will I say if someone challenges or disrespects this boundary?

Practice with a friend or in front of a mirror to build confidence. (you are not crazy if you do that; MJ, the king of pop, used to rehearse in front of the mirror all night)

<u>Step 4</u>: Put your boundaries into practice and maintain them. Ask yourself:

- What small steps can I take today to honor this boundary?
- How will I handle situations where this boundary is tested?
- Track Your Progress: Keep a journal or chart to reflect on your experiences, what's working, and what might need adjustment.

<u>Step 5:</u> Recognize that boundaries may need to evolve, and that's okay. Ask yourself:

- How are these boundaries serving me?
- What adjustments might be needed?
- How can I make those changes while staying true to my values?

<u>Step 6:</u> Keep your boundaries aligned with your growth and changing circumstances. For reflection, ask yourself:

- What has changed in my life, and how might that affect my boundaries?
- Where have I succeeded, and what challenges have I faced?
- Update and refine your boundaries to ensure they continue to serve you.

Exercise 14.1: Looking Forward

Step 1: Embrace the doubt, embrace the uncertainty.
- What exactly are you doubting about your decision?
- Is there a pattern in your life where doubt has arisen before?
- Can you name the emotions linked to this doubt?

Step 2: Dig into the root of this doubt, and define the source of the doubt.
- What expectations might be causing this doubt?
- Is there an external influence (like societal pressures or peer opinions) affecting how you feel?
- How does this decision align or misalign with your Authenticity Pyramid© (beliefs, motives, values, passions, abilities, purpose, and mission)?

Step 3: Revisit the decision process and reflect on how you arrived at this decision.
- What were the pros and cons you considered?
- What values and priorities guided your choice?
- Did you consult others, follow intuition, or rely on facts? How did those elements influence the final decision?

Step 4: Explore alternative scenarios and consider what might have happened if you chose differently.
- What are the potential outcomes of a different decision?
- How would those outcomes align with your values and goals?
- How do you feel when you think about these alternative paths?

Step 5: Focus on learning and growth, and shift your perspective to view this experience as an opportunity.
- What have you learned about yourself through this decision and its aftermath?
- How can this doubt or regret become a tool for growth?
- What skills or insights can you carry into future decisions?

Step 6: Practice self-compassion

- What would you tell a friend in the same situation?
- How can you treat yourself with the same empathy and understanding?
- How does self-compassion help ease the weight of doubt?

Step 7: If needed, decide if something needs to be done and take constructive action
- Is there a concrete action that can be taken to address a real problem stemming from the decision?
- What are the possible consequences of this action?
- How will this action align with your goals and values?

Step 8: Accept the decision and move forward.
- How can you consciously choose to accept your decision and its consequences?
- What strategies can help you let go of lingering doubts?
- How can you celebrate the courage it took to make this decision?

Exercise 14.2: Mistakes Analysis

Step 1: Identify the Mistake
- What exactly went wrong?
- Why do you consider it a mistake?
- What were your original goals and intentions?
- How did the outcome differ from what you expected?
- What are your feelings about this mistake?

Step 2: Analyze the Causes
- What were the contributing factors to this mistake?
- Did you have all the necessary information?
- Were there any external pressures that influenced your decision?
- Did cognitive biases play a role? If so, which ones?

Step 3: Assess the Impact
- What were the immediate consequences of this mistake?
- What long-term effects has it caused or might it cause?
- Who else has been affected by this mistake, and how?
- What opportunities have been lost or gained?

Step 4: Explore Alternative Actions
- What could you have done differently?
- What information would have been helpful to have?
- What alternative solutions might have been available?
- If you were in the same situation again, what would you do?

Step 5: Develop a Corrective Plan
- What specific steps can you take to correct this mistake?
- What resources will you need?
- How will you measure success in correcting the mistake?
- What timeline will you follow?

Step 6: Implement the Plan
- How will you initiate the corrective action?
- What support or collaboration will you need?
- How will you monitor progress?
- What will you do if challenges arise during implementation?

Step 7: Reflect and Integrate Learning
- What have you learned from this process?
- How will this experience influence future decisions?
- What strategies will you employ to avoid similar mistakes?
- How have you grown or changed as a result?

www.ingramcontent.com/pod-product-compliance
Lightning Source LLC
Chambersburg PA
CBHW030859310526
45786CB00019B/2067